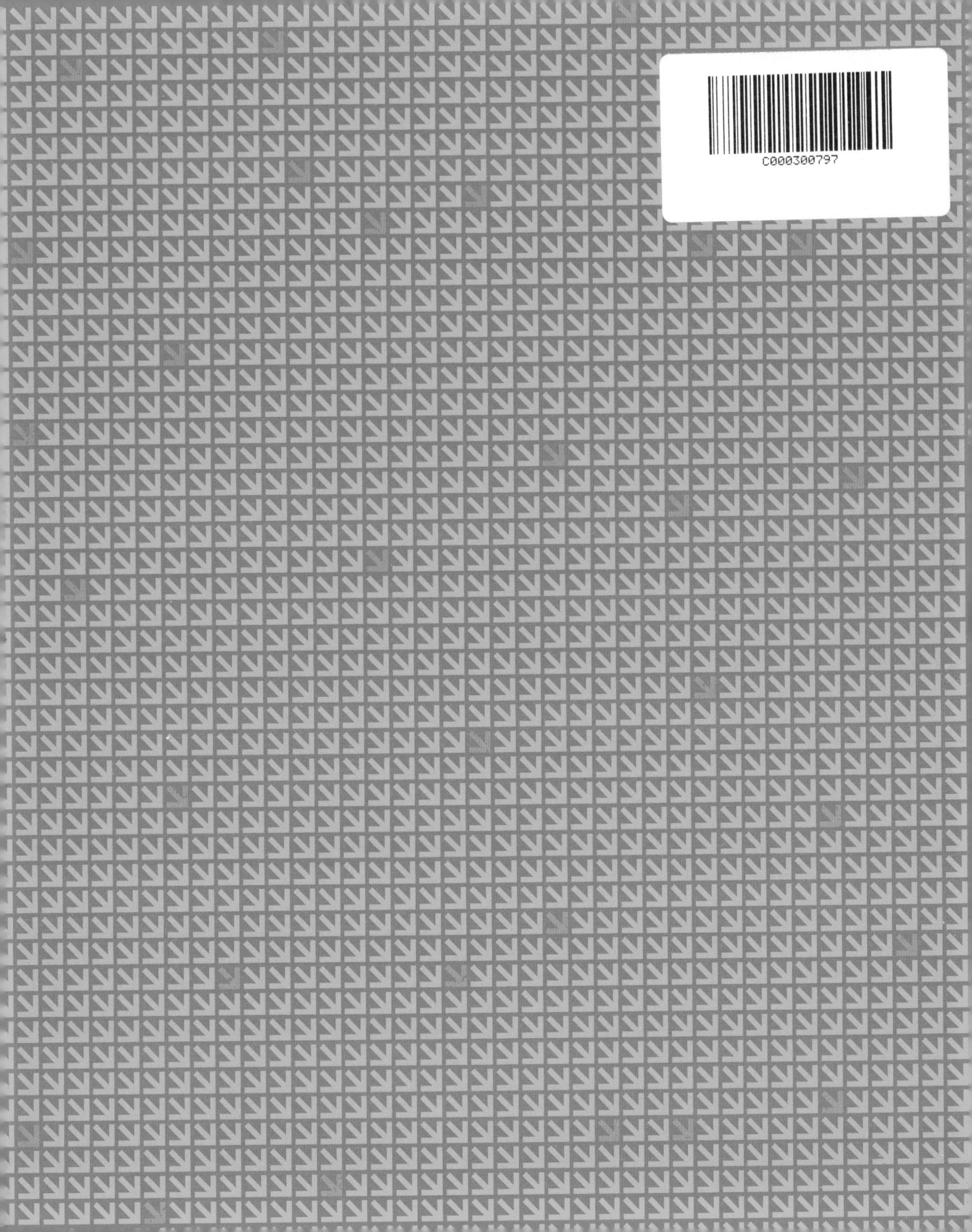

RED SIXTY SEVEN

A collection of words and art inspired by Britain's most vulnerable birds. Curated by Kit Jewitt

First published in the United Kingdom in 2020 by the British Trust for Ornithology,
The Nunnery, Thetford, Norfolk, IP24 2PU. www.bto.org

This book was produced by BTO Services Ltd on behalf of the British Trust for Ornithology,
Registered Charity Number 216652 (England & Wales), SC039193 (Scotland).

Design: Stew Graham www.graphic-stew.co.uk / Layout: Mike Toms
Proofreading: Jamie Dunning, Viola Ross-Smith

ISBN 978–1–912642–13–7

Printed and bound in Italy by Printer Trento, an FSC® certified company for printing books on FSC mixed papers in compliance with the chain of custody and on-product labelling standards. Printer Trento has an ISO 14001 certified environmental management system.

RED SIXTY SEVEN

Curated by Kit Jewitt

Foreword

Have you ever had an idea pop into your head and, without thinking, blurted it out loud on Twitter and then been compelled to go through with it? It happens to me, or rather it happens to my online alter-ego YOLOBirder, a lot. The first time I'd gone off half-cocked like this, I ended up with 400 T-shirts to post!

The second time resulted in *#99Birds*: a collection of original bird artworks, lovingly bound into a unique one-of-a-kind book. Sold at auction, it raised over £3,000 for bird conservation. This was a project forged on social media and made possible only by the kindness of 99 talented, like-minded strangers. It provided a brief, welcome antidote to the division engulfing society at the time, a time when our natural world was, and still is, under relentless siege. It was a joyous thing but, ultimately, the impact was but a drop in our microplastics-filled oceans.

Detailing the declines of bird populations in the UK, Birds of Conservation Concern – the UK Red List – highlights that one in four UK bird species is now under significant threat, with 20 new species being added to the list in 2015. Birds that we consider common and may take for granted, like House Sparrow and Starling, Herring Gull and Song Thrush, are more vulnerable than ever before. In my lifetime alone it is estimated that 40–50 million birds have vanished from our skies. It is a harrowing, depressing read, but can also be seen as a rally cry, a call-to-arms. It made me want to do something, no matter how small, and gave me an idea for another book.

The idea was simple; a book featuring the 67 Red-listed birds, each illustrated by a different artist with a personal story from a diverse collection of writers. And every penny from sales donated directly to Red-listed species conservation projects run by BTO and RSPB. All that remained was the small task of persuading 134 people to contribute. And to give their work, including the 67 original artworks, to the project, for free*. So once again I took to Twitter. And once again the generosity of people, most of whom I have never met, was simply staggering and I cannot thank each and every one of them enough.

Red Sixty Seven is the result; 67 love letters to our most vulnerable species, each beautifully illustrated by some of the best wildlife artists around, showcasing a range of styles as varied as the birds in these pages. My hope is that the book will bring the Red List to a wider audience whilst raising funds for the charities working to help the birds most at need.

Kit Jewitt, December 2019

*To maximise the fundraising the 67 original artworks are being sold too, as 67 equally priced and affordable 'lucky dip' blind lots.

UNDERSTANDING THE BIRDS OF CONSERVATION CONCERN (BOCC) CRITERIA

As Mark Eaton notes in his introduction, BOCC assessments use a strict set of quantitative criteria to examine the status of all of the UK's 'regularly' occurring species. Each of the 67 species accounts is accompanied by a summary of its changing BOCC status over the four assessments carried out to date – labelled 1 to 4 and colour-coded to denote the list (Red, Amber or Green) on which it was placed during that assessment.

Also shown are the Red List criteria applicable to the species during the most recent (fourth) assessment. These relate to whether or not the species is listed as being 'Globally Threatened' on the IUCN Red List; whether there has been an historical decline in the breeding population; a more recent decline in the breeding population; a decline in the non-breeding population; a decline in breeding range; or a decline in non-breeding range. Where any of these criteria was met during the most recent assessment the dot is coloured red.

Introduction

Mark Eaton

It's a rather sad but maybe inevitable fact that we are far short of all the resources we need to conserve the UK's nature – to arrest the declining trajectory, and to help our wildlife populations return to former levels.

Whilst public support for conservation continues to grow, as evidenced by a 20% increase in NGO expenditure on biodiversity conservation over just five years, funding from governments has crashed. Public sector spending on biodiversity in the UK has fallen by 42% as a proportion of GDP since 2008/09. The football team I support has an annual turnover bigger than the total spent by UK and devolved governments on conservation. It's not just governments: as a society, we don't place sufficient significance upon our natural world.

The consequence of this is that conservationists don't have the funding to work on everything they want, everywhere, all the time. We have to prioritise to make the most effective use of the available resources, to make sure every penny counts. Typically, this is done in two ways – by identifying the best places for nature, and by identifying the species that most need our help (these two approaches don't work in isolation – often the best places are identified by virtue of the species they hold). The latter is where 'red-listing' – formal processes to identify the species most deserving of help – comes in.

The standard approach for species assessments across the world is to assess the risk of species going extinct, using the International Union for Conservation of Nature's (IUCN) Red List approach. Initially only applicable to global assessments, this can now be done at a regional or national level, and for many taxonomic groups assessments of extinction risk have been made at the British scale: we know that 15% of the species assessed are considered at risk of extinction. However, for birds in the UK we use a home-grown Birds of Conservation Concern (BOCC) system, which considers a broader range of issues than simply the risk of extinction.

BOCC assessments use a strict set of quantitative criteria to examine the status of all of the UK's 'regularly' occurring species (scarce migrants and vagrants aren't considered), and uses a simple traffic light system to classify them. There are 'Red' criteria with thresholds for rates of decline in numbers and range, historical decline and international threat (if a species is considered globally threatened it is automatically Red-listed in the UK), and 'Amber' criteria with lower thresholds for the same trend measures, and a range of other considerations such as rarity, international importance of UK populations, and how localised a species is. If a species meets any of the Red List criteria it goes onto the Red List; if it doesn't, but meets any Amber List criterion, it is Amber-listed; and if it doesn't meet any of the criteria it is Green-listed. We have attempted to keep the criteria the same between the four assessments conducted to date, but there have been a few necessary tweaks to adapt to changing circumstances and data sources.

Assessments are conducted by a panel of experts drawn from ornithological NGOs and governmental conservation agencies, and make use of the huge wealth of data we have on bird numbers, distributions, and trends thanks to the efforts of thousands of volunteer surveyors and recorders.

The most recent review, BOCC4, was published in the journal *British Birds* in December 2015, and is available online. Like the previous three reviews, it made for sobering reading, with a substantial jump in the Red List: 67 species were Red-listed, 27.5% of the 244 species assessed and 15 more than ever before. Twenty species moved onto the Red List and three species, Wryneck, Temminck's Stint and Serin, were moved to the list of 'former breeders' – extinct, in other words.

As well as highlighting individual concern for the 67 Red-listed species, BOCC assessments tells us about some of the broader patterns in the UK environment. The new arrivals on the BOCC4 Red List included five upland birds, reflecting growing concerns about the impact of intensive grazing, drainage, and burning in this habitat. Three newly Red-listed seabirds, Puffin, Shag and Kittiwake, joined Herring Gull and Arctic Skua in sounding an alarm about the state of our seas. No less than 16 woodland birds are now Red-listed, although proportionately, farmland birds are the hardest hit with 12 on the list, and numbers of Red-listed farmland birds such as Corn Bunting and Turtle Dove continue to plummet. The latter species also points to another issue – of 50 species classified as long-distance Afro-Palearctic migrants, 21 are now Red-listed.

The good news came through the down-listing from Red to Amber of three species – Dunlin, Bittern and Nightjar – with the change in the latter two reflecting population recoveries in response to dedicated conservation action. They follow in the footsteps of Stone-curlew, Woodlark, Marsh Harrier and Red Kite in escaping the Red List – indeed, the latter has now made it to the Green List. Whilst the Red List continues to grow, these demonstrate that we do know how to turn things around: if only we had the resources…

Mark Eaton, RSPB

THE SIXTY SEVEN

White-fronted Goose

Anser albifrons

CHANGING BOCC STATUS 1–2–3–4

RED-LIST CRITERIA APPLICABLE

- IUCN Globally Threatened
- Historical breeding population decline
- Breeding population decline
- Non-breeding population decline
- Breeding range decline
- Non-breeding range decline

She is feather, blood and bone.

Two million years of evolution.
Two million revolutions around the sun.

Hers is a story of deep time, told wing-bound, above lands forged from ice and fire, above a world folding and moulding to glacial ebb and flow.
Hers is a story told in slow time.

This Greenland summer has seen her new brood hatch and grow. Her proud gaggle follows her, tail-waggling and beak-nibbling on the arctic tundra. A family, feeding and fattening. Her old flight feathers are frayed and worn. They are discarded, fluttering to the wind. Brand new ones are pushing through, bursting from their sheaths to be oiled and preened. They are light enough to carry her skyward and strong enough to ride the wildest storms. Wings wide, she tests the wind, ready for the journey hard-wired into her memory.

For she is a traveller of the ancient sky-roads, along flight-lines woven like thread into the pattern of this landscape.

As the first snow flurries fall, she will rise above the ice cap and angle her wings towards the southern sky, stopping to rest and refuel on the Icelandic lowlands, and then on, to her ancestral Scottish home of Islay. She will descend, her discordant cries calling to her family, bonding them to each other, binding them to this place. She will overwinter here, on these warm, wet Celtic fringes, until the world tilts once more towards the sun, bringing the summer and the tailwinds to take her north again.

But hers has become a story of our time, of wetlands drained and claimed by man. The pattern of our climate is altering. The world is warming up and melting, changing the very land she depends upon. The great skeins of her kind that once filled our skies are vanishing. This is the tale of the Anthropocene, where change, too fast, is happening.
The fabric of her landscape is rapidly unravelling.

Two million revolutions around the sun
Two million years of evolution,

Undone.

WORDS – GILL LEWIS | **ART –** SZABOLCS KÓKAY

Pochard

Aythya ferina

Apparently, one of my first intelligible utterances as a very young Dilger was "duck", and I very much doubt that I was the only toddler who learnt this word alongside the more familiar vocalisations of "mamma", "dadda" and "dog" during my earliest years.

Now living close to Chew Valley Lake in the West Country, there is one duck species that I'll always look forward to catching up with more than any other, as the year winds down and temperatures plummet. The male Pochard's chestnut head, laser-beam red eye and black breast make it instantly identifiable; each time I 'scope up' one of these wonderful little ducks the word 'smart' pops into my mind. Being a diving duck, you might expect to be constantly playing a game of 'now you see me, now you don't' when attempting to spot this species. However, due to the Pochard's preference for feeding at night, this frequently leaves the day for little more than loafing around at the surface, enabling them to be enjoyed at leisure by 'duck-philes' like me.

Despite the vast majority of Pochard only visiting here in winter, the creation of reservoirs and flooding of gravel pits has encouraged a small and burgeoning population to now remain in the UK year-round. This is both welcome news and at least some recompense to counterbalance the worrying trend of a steady decline in overwintering numbers since the 1990s. Exactly why our winter waterbodies are being graced by far fewer Pochard remains unclear, but the ever-present menace of climate change is undoubtedly a major factor. The Pochard is just one of a whole suite of migratory species now 'short-stopping' in ever greater numbers, as they shorten their autumn migration to spend the winter closer to their traditional breeding grounds in northern and eastern Europe. Research on the Continent also seems to indicate the decline of Black-headed Gull colonies across northern Europe, which Pochard nest in amongst for protection, and the explosion in populations of predatory American Mink across many wetland sites can't be helping either.

I will concede that of all our threatened bird species, the more glamorous and charismatic species, such as Puffin and Cuckoo, will undoubtedly grab the headlines. But, I'd argue, a winter without spotting a Pochard would be even worse than Christmas without turkey.

CHANGING BOCC STATUS 1–2–3–4

RED-LIST CRITERIA APPLICABLE

- IUCN Globally Threatened
- Historical breeding population decline
- Breeding population decline
- Non-breeding population decline
- Breeding range decline
- Non-breeding range decline

WORDS – MIKE DILGER | **ART –** ADELE POUND

3

Scaup

Aythya marila

The Scaup's presence in our country is not much more than a flirtation. This duck is already wedded to the vast swathes of open tundra that sweep across the Northern Hemisphere and, in winter, to temperate marine shallows mainly to the east and west of us. Our breeding population is all but extinct, and in autumn and winter there can be more birds in a single flock across the Atlantic than in the whole of Britain.

The last time I saw one was on a small inland lake of no great importance. It was a male swimming amidst a flock of Tufted Ducks and Pochards, as if it was the love child of the two, on a cold, inconsequential January morning. It was a typical Scaup meeting, something that raises eyebrows rather than blood pressure. The Scaup isn't rare and it certainly isn't beautiful. In Britain it is defined by what it isn't: not the two toned Tufted, nor the tricoloured (male) Pochard, but somewhere in between, the unappreciated middle child diving duck.

And yet the Scaup is magnificent. It is a tough, powerful seaduck that can cope with extreme cold and turbulent water. It is renowned as a swift, powerful flier, much speedier than a dabbling duck, and large flocks are celebrated for their habit of twisting and shifting in flight, often making tadpole shapes with a mass of birds at the front and some tailing behind. They form large flocks on the sea, too, dotted all over the water. Where they are common, Scaup are thrilling.

The Scaup should really be referred to as the Greater Scaup, because there is a Lesser Scaup across the Atlantic. The Greater Scaup is the only member of its group that has conquered both the Old World and the New; Tufted Ducks and Pochards have not. That, in itself, is also an impressive feat.

So, the Scaup that I saw on my lake was hardly representative of the impressive bird it really is – a fish out of water on the water, you might say. Where they are common, they also prefer to stay in flocks with their own kind, so again my Scaup was on the edge, mixing with other diving ducks.

I expected it to move away, soon, and it duly obliged. The Greater Scaup effected the Great Escape, back to somewhere appropriate.

CHANGING BOCC STATUS 1–2–3–4

RED-LIST CRITERIA APPLICABLE

- IUCN Globally Threatened
- Historical breeding population decline
- Breeding population decline
- Non-breeding population decline
- Breeding range decline
- Non-breeding range decline

WORDS – DOMINIC COUZENS | **ART –** DAFILA SCOTT

Long-tailed Duck

Clangula hyemalis

CHANGING BOCC STATUS 1–2–3–4

RED-LIST CRITERIA APPLICABLE

- IUCN Globally Threatened
- Historical breeding population decline
- Breeding population decline
- Non-breeding population decline
- Breeding range decline
- Non-breeding range decline

Blown out beyond the tumbling ramparts of the tempest, they roll into the churn and suck of raw water and squat in the swallows of spray, spin up with the spindrift and vanish into black canyons behind slashing veils of spume.

As the colossal swells sink they speck the sea-green, freckle the foam and slip over the crush of breakers, skittish in the squall, spots of flotsam on the ocean's roiling hell. And when moonless night clamps down on the maelstrom they vanish from the earth and become mythical, like medieval beasts whose veracity is impossible to reconcile.

They come from the north and gather in our distance; when the wind licks their voices we think we hear dogs braying beyond the rollers, their garrulous crooning swirls like the Norse, drowning on the edge of our earshot. Our salt-slapped cheeks trickle tears as we strain our eyes to see these sirens, out there in the death zone, and if the storm lulls they come to us, come to us, slowly on the tide, still beyond the rocks, far off our beach.

Up they bob, throwing their heads back and forth to sink into the ink in some strange synchrony, and in that cramping cold they gobble cockles and clams to grind in their gizzards; gobies, sticklebacks and cod slip into their pink-bridged bills. And closer they confirm their clean beauty, piebald and chocolate, with delicate eye-rings and cocky crowns, and when the gale whips up their whip-tails they arch over their backs and give the 'V' to the sea.

They belong to the Baltic, are born of the Arctic, but if you slip on seaweed on the eastern shores, in winter they may be yours. I got closest on a Dornoch dawn in the nineties; they were in the surf, almost within reach. And then I tumbled over a greasy dock to grab a strandline corpse from which I plucked the long tail. And as we drove away I teased those plumes to form a perfect treasure; some fragment of an enigma, some tangible confirmation that a creature on the brink of my belief lives out there, where waves drown dreams and kill men, where only legends live long and their tales longer.

WORDS – CHRIS PACKHAM | **ART –** CHRIS PACKHAM

Chris Packham 2019

Common Scoter

Melanitta nigra

CHANGING BOCC STATUS 1-2-3-4

RED-LIST CRITERIA APPLICABLE

- IUCN Globally Threatened
- Historical breeding population decline
- Breeding population decline
- Non-breeding population decline
- Breeding range decline
- Non-breeding range decline

Mercurial flocks of Common Scoter, the archetypal seaduck, are a defining feature of the grey vastness of Liverpool Bay. Beyond the amusements of Blackpool, over 10% of the north-west European population winters across an arc from Morecambe to Anglesey.

Years ago, I was involved in boat-based Scoter surveys, investigating how planned wind farm developments might affect the species. Only from the sea, or the air, can one come to terms with the size of these vast amorphous Scoter slicks, and hence an understanding of the importance of this coast for the species. Scientific careers are not geographically fickle however, and shortly after, I was absented from those shores for over a decade in the rainforests of Brazil. Fate and Amazonia would yet rekindle my relationship with Common Scoter. After returning to the UK to take up a permanent academic post, and having acquired a set of sound recorders for use in the rainforest, I deployed one in my garden in the Peak District. My interest in monitoring nocturnal bird migration – termed 'nocmigging' – had been kindled at Cornell University in the US; in September 2017, upon examining recordings, I was pleasantly surprised to find a series of whistles and wing whirrs. A flock of Scoter had passed over our house in the early hours. Success!

Moving house a little further north to Hadfield, I found more evidence of Scoter, and indeed of quite substantial waterbird movements. Working at home late on 21 March 2018 I had forgotten to put the recorder out, a serendipitous lapse that led to one of the most exciting hours of birding I have ever had, anywhere. Opening the back door at 10.15 pm I was greeted by a veritable wall of Common Scoter and Redwing calls. Running upstairs to get my wife Nárgila out of bed, we sat outside in awe as the avian contents of Liverpool Bay emptied over our Peak District garden. Wave after wave of Scoter passed, along with myriad thrushes, wildfowl and waders. The weather was poor, visibility down to a few hundred meters with light rain and south-westerly winds, favourable to onward migration but also responsible for pushing birds low through the Longdendale Valley; the trans-Pennine leg of their adventurous migration back to boreal breeding grounds. A scout of the numerous local reservoirs the next day revealed not a Scoter in sight! A once in a lifetime event? Nope. In similar conditions on the 19 March 2019 a nocturnal river of Scoter again flowed east over our house. After rapid telecommunications, the event was shared with other local birders enabling them to furnish their garden lists with an unseen seaduck! Fifty thousand or more Scoter might ply this route twice a year...

WORDS – ALEXANDER LEES | **ART –** RAY SCALLY

6 Velvet Scoter

Melanitta fusca

CHANGING BOCC STATUS 1–2–3–4

RED-LIST CRITERIA APPLICABLE

- IUCN Globally Threatened
- Historical breeding population decline
- Breeding population decline
- Non-breeding population decline
- Breeding range decline
- Non-breeding range decline

I started my sea-watching apprenticeship under the wing of Fran Evans at St. Abb's in the Scottish Borders. Fran was as sharp-eyed as they come, and I learned a lot from her in those early years.

The reason I loved sea-watching so much was its unpredictability. You can study all the weather maps you like, but you never really know what you are going to see on any given day. I remember some amazing days sat on the rocks at the end of the headland. Streams of skuas and shearwaters passing by, each aiding identification by its flight pattern and shape. Although these birds were exciting to see, it was the seaduck that I was particularly interested in. For me, these fast fliers were usually difficult to get onto, to track and identify, on a sea-watch; particularly those that were out at a distance. However, with a bit of practice and experience I was soon identifying Wigeon, Teal, Long-tailed Duck, and Common Scoter with ease; these being the most common ducks observed during a sea-watch, at certain times of year at least. There was one duck I was keen to see, the Velvet Scoter. This was a scarce species off the headland.

One calm spring morning, the sea-watching didn't look promising at all. It was a beautiful day and the sea was flat calm. I decided to set up my telescope nonetheless and see what I could find. Besides the local breeding seabirds and a few distant Northern Gannets there was not much to see. However, after an hour or so I locked onto four distant ducks. I kept on them and as they flew closer I could see that the front three were Common Scoter. The fourth duck seemed larger and thicker-necked compared to the nearby Common Scoter. I kept my eye glued to this bird and I could soon see it had a gleaming white secondary bar. It continued to fly close in towards me and the bright sun caught the extensive bright yellow on its bill and white crescent under the eye. I could not believe I was getting such incredible views of my first Velvet Scoter at my favourite location.

This first observation of Velvet Scoter will always be special to me but, even though I have seen hundreds since, I will never tire of seeing this spectacular seaduck.

WORDS – TRISTAN REID | **ART –** JACKIE GARNER

GARNER

7

Black Grouse

Lyrurus tetrix

CHANGING BOCC STATUS 1–2–3–4

RED-LIST CRITERIA APPLICABLE

- IUCN Globally Threatened
- Historical breeding population decline
- Breeding population decline
- Non-breeding population decline
- Breeding range decline
- Non-breeding range decline

It is hard not to anthropomorphise the wonderfully ridiculous lek of the Black Grouse. Males with their chests puffed out, their tails spread to make themselves look as big as possible, making the loudest noise they can, irresistibly remind me of the bar of an Australian pub near closing time. That the males have no part in making the nest or rearing the young only makes the comparison feel more apt.

Yet this isn't a reflection on humans, but a reminder of the sophisticated, complicated lives of so many of the creatures around us that we seldom see. A reminder of how evolution works in truly weird and wonderful ways.

This is something I should be able to see, not far from my home in Sheffield. I owe it to the Manchester-based academic Dr Alexander Lees for drawing my attention to a site on the Staffordshire moors, Swallow Moss, only 30 miles from home, where a solidly stone-built hide was erected to facilitate watching Black Grouse lekking.

Yet this is a story of absence, not discovery, for the hide is now boarded up, a small and sad tribute to the fate of yet another Red-listed species in grave danger of disappearing from our nation.

It isn't hard to see why the Black Grouse chose this site, a nearby tangled woodland, some boggy ground where a pipe carries a stream from it onto reed-choked pasture. And for the twitcher, a magnificent view over a rolling valley of emerald-green rye-grass crosshatched with stone walls, picturesquely dotted with Belted Galloways and Scottish Blackface, means it must have been the perfect dales location for a leisurely brew after the Black Grouse show was over.

There were once many such sites in England, if not usually so perfectly picturesque. In the 18th century, when Gilbert White saw lekking in Hampshire, it was a common bird, yet it now stands with so many others as quite likely on its way out of our landscapes.

My knowledge of the lek comes solely from YouTube videos – and in our incredibly nature-depleted landscapes that's increasingly all most people will see of our wildlife.

We're known as a nation of animal lovers, but the silent, still ground of Swallow Moss tells another story – of a nation that's failed to manage its land for all of its inhabitants, that needs to radically change its approach to land, for people, and planet, and the Black Grouse.

WORDS – NATALIE BENNETT | **ART –** HOWARD GRAY

8

Capercaillie

Tetrao urogallus

CHANGING BOCC STATUS 1–2–3–4

RED-LIST CRITERIA APPLICABLE

- IUCN Globally Threatened
- Historical breeding population decline
- Breeding population decline
- Non-breeding population decline
- Breeding range decline
- Non-breeding range decline

You see them on YouTube, strutting around the lek-site like hedge-fund managers high on profit, cocksure of themselves in front of the womenfolk, making those ridiculous sounds like marbles dropping through a marble run and a ratchet tightening a rope.

With lush blue-black plumage, a curious white ellipse on each scapular and a red brow, the male holds his tail feathers erect like a lacquered fan. Female Capercaillie are entirely different; the head and wings are barred silver and grey, like stag's horn lichen garlanding the forest's branches. And like sunlight on pine bark, a flush of sienna spreads across the upper breast and neck. There could have been half a dozen females perched in the canopy that morning, and we'd have been none the wiser. Their diet is of pine needles, buds and in summer, berries from the forest floor.

Together with guide Simon Pawsey, I walked into one of the last Strathspey refuges, though it was hardly remote. Signs at the gate asked walkers, dog-walkers and bikers to keep to the paths. Only 20 minutes in, something immense and dark – a Hercules plane of a bird – flew over the canopy, blotting out the steel-cold sky. A few minutes later and with an explosive crack, a second male burst out of the heather and blaeberry metres from the path. Dazed into stillness, I saw how it swivelled between the trees before breaking across open ground. Then, at the terminus of that one isolated pocket of forest, the caper flew back into his territory; hugely, soundlessly. And here's the rub; capers don't travel in search of a mate. What that open ground represented was fragmentation and consequential loss.

Just 1,100 Capercaillie remain in the last stronghold of Strathspey. But we have been here before; capers were wiped from the UK during the 1700s. In 1837, Swedish birds were reintroduced to Perthshire, and the species thrived, expanding its range across much of Scotland to 20,000 birds. Their more recent losses speak of habitat destruction, climate change, predation, collisions with fencing, disturbance.

But hope lies ahead. The Cairngorms landscape is being restored on an epic scale. Here, as elsewhere, a bridge of young pines has been inserted between that one section of mature forest and the next. The bright green youngsters bristled against a horizon of snowy mountains. By re-connecting these forest pockets, our Capercaillie may just survive to strut another day.

WORDS – KAREN LLOYD | **ART –** CAROLINE DALY

Grey Partridge

Perdix perdix

CHANGING BOCC STATUS 1–2–3–4

RED-LIST CRITERIA APPLICABLE
- IUCN Globally Threatened
- Historical breeding population decline
- Breeding population decline
- Non-breeding population decline
- Breeding range decline
- Non-breeding range decline

Even now I listen for a kind of echo of them as I walk up Lightwood Road, in Buxton, Derbyshire, where I was born. Yet I cannot recall when I last actually heard Grey Partridges here. They've gone. And I miss them more every passing year with something like a physical ache.

Partridge calls were part of the soundtrack to my childhood. It is a bird vocalisation like no other, except perhaps that other instructive casualty of agricultural change, the Corncrake. It is minimal, mechanical, un-avian. It has a creaking quality said to resemble the sound of an old gate swinging on rusty hinges, with emphasis on the opening portion followed by a long trailing slur: "*Ké-e-e-e-e-e-e-r, ké-e-e-e-e-e-e-r, ké-e-e-e-e-e-r*". Over and over.

No transcription, however, can give a sense of its wonderfully bowed, echoic, spartan, pleading, memory-enriched quality, nor of the power of the sound, as night falls on those late-winter hills, to merge with that light and that air to awaken a synaesthetic emotional effect. It is as if the dusk itself has found voice. It seemed to me then like a bigger door, a larger opening, a newer life were all being prised open by the bird's yearning note. If I hear one now my heart aches with the joy of it. And the sad remembrance.

Grey Partridges have performed what is, in many ways, a late version of the Corncrake's own disappearing act earlier in the same century. There were once millions of Grey Partridges in this country. Today there are about 75,000. For centuries it was the pre-eminent sporting bird of the farmed environment in lowland Britain. Come St. Partridge's Day, on 1 September, the English country house and all its multiple cultural meanings were inflected towards *Perdix perdix*. The pre-Second World War bag was two million birds. There was an occasion in late October 1887 at the Grange in Hampshire where seven guns killed 4,075 Grey Partridges over four consecutive days. There was a time in Norfolk at Warham on the Holkham estate, where I spent the summer of 1985, when eight guns downed 1,671 of them.

But let's not recall Grey Partridge as a victim of anally retentive sportsmen. Let's remind ourselves of the living mystery. I can see them on the Lightwood hillside, just at the horizon, where the field contour meets the March evening sky, and there are Lapwings calling and a Mistle Thrush has come to sing from a high Beech at last light; and there they are: four squat dark spheres, devoid of colour, one with neck craned and out of its beak, held wide, comes that glorious curving rainbow of sound. And the land speaks again.

WORDS – MARK COCKER | **ART –** KITTIE JONES

10

Balearic Shearwater

Puffinus mauretanicus

The Balearic Shearwater is one of the most inconspicuous and scarce seabirds regularly passing through UK waters. To the untrained eye the species can look strikingly similar to the much more frequently encountered Manx Shearwater, a closely related and local breeding species. Both are medium-sized seabirds belonging to the tubenoses, a group of long-lived birds that also includes albatrosses and petrels, and known to travel vast distances with ease by utilising local winds to soar across the sea.

Being able to reach distant places effortlessly explains the presence of Balearic Shearwaters in UK waters, migrating through our region in autumn and winter, after breeding on islands in the Mediterranean. During the breeding season, birds tend to return with the same partner to the same island each year to raise a single chick over multiple months. Incubation and chick-rearing duties are shared to allow both parents to restore their energy reserves between incubation shifts and to undertake provisioning trips to feed their chick.

The time at their breeding grounds is also when the birds are most vulnerable to numerous human-caused threats, such as being caught as by-catch in fisheries, being predated by invasive mammals, or losing habitat to tourism developments. In conjunction with less localised pressures, such as overfishing and climate change, these have led to a dramatic decline in Balearic Shearwater numbers over recent decades and resulted in the species being classified as 'Critically Endangered' by the IUCN. However, the secretive nocturnal lifestyle they exhibit when returning to their breeding colonies, together with a tendency to nest in hidden burrows and caves, makes it hard to accurately monitor the remaining population. Current estimates predict that only as few as 2,000 breeding pairs could be left in the world.

It is exciting to look through your scope while sitting in your favourite sea-watching spot on the UK coast and to notice a less contrast-rich, greyish-brown shearwater, with a plump body and extended feet, soaring rather nervously between the waves. Just make sure to completely and entirely convince yourself it was a Balearic Shearwater before it is gone, to shut down any external or internal sceptics. After all, no one knows how many more opportunities you will have to doubt yourself about this familiar-looking stranger.

CHANGING BOCC STATUS 1–2–3–4

RED-LIST CRITERIA APPLICABLE
- ● IUCN Globally Threatened
- ● Historical breeding population decline
- ● Breeding population decline
- ● Non-breeding population decline
- ● Breeding range decline
- ● Non-breeding range decline

WORDS – SASKIA WISCHNEWSKI | **ART –** SUZY SHARPE

Shag

Phalacrocorax aristotelis

I grew up on the Norfolk coast and often felt my life was defined by living on edges. The edge of geography, where relentlessly flat land met the endless expanse of big Norfolk skies. The edge of environments, sometimes spending as much time in the turbid waters of the North Sea as I did on land. The edge of comfort, where biting Arctic winds comforted me no less than the caressing summer sun.

I used to feel that no one knew my beach like I did. I walked it daily with my dog, Toby. We would walk miles and leave this turbulent but calming, frigid yet cathartic realm of edges with a sense of wholeness that I had not known before or since.

I had endless fascination for those animals which lived in this realm of ephemeral edges. Porpoises momentarily gliding from their world to mine, as they broke the surface, and fiery-eyed swimming crabs stranded high up along the tideline filled me with a sense of wonder. Then one day I found a body. It was at the water's edge and was untouched by decay. I bent down to scoop it up and marvelled at the shimmering feathers. I used to watch Shags flying by, out to sea. They fired my imagination and admiration for being, like me, experts at living on the edge, flying so close to the sea sometimes it was as if they were only ever moments away from flying underwater. I would see them on calm days close inshore, their little black feet kicking in the air as they dived under for sand eels.

But they seemed unreal to me. Only existing in clear, coloured detail in books or in near-blurred obscurity along my shoreline. But here we were, Toby and I, examining a glistening emerald and amethystine wonder. I was able to finally see a Shag for the first time. I can still remember the reptilian scales along its feet, endless hues of greens, blues and violets and a perfectly-sculpted, hooked beak. I had read they have green eyes, so I touched a finger ever so gently against its eyelid and remember my breath catching at the sheer beauty. As sad as I was that this beautiful bird was dead, I felt a huge sense of privilege at my intimate glimpse into the life of this bird which thrives on the edge. Even now, when I see one, regardless of how near or far away it is, I always see that impossibly green, beautiful eye.

CHANGING BOCC STATUS 1–2–3–4

RED-LIST CRITERIA APPLICABLE
- IUCN Globally Threatened
- Historical breeding population decline
- Breeding population decline
- Non-breeding population decline
- Breeding range decline
- Non-breeding range decline

WORDS – BEN GARROD | **ART –** WYNONA LEGG

W. LEGG

Red-necked Grebe

Podiceps grisegena

There used to be benches here, but the wooden slats are long gone and now only the concrete frames remain. A crumbling shelter in a fading seaside town. I'm early enough to get pole position, tucking my folding chair in to the corner to escape the worst of the north-westerly. There's a faint tang of urine; remember not to put my flask on the floor.

With sunrise the sky brightens – as much as a stormy October day can – enough to see small groups of Teal and Wigeon already heading west. They're low, often disappearing in the swell. Other birders arrive, "Much moving?" the seawatchers' hello. The waves crashing on the rock breakwaters below are already sending sheets of spray across the front of the shelter. Off-white lumps of spume float by like erratically thrown custard pies. Still two hours until high tide – might get wet feet today. The cartwheeling wind turbines disappear as the first of the day's squalls barrels in, bringing with it a gang of Kittiwakes – no brown mantles in this lot. Small groups of Northern Gannets start streaming east, seemingly every bird a different age.

A startled "Oh, sorry" announces a family as they get blown round the corner of the shelter. Their shorts and T-shirts to our waterproof trousers, coats, hats and gloves. More squalls bring three bonxies close in, crossing paths with lines of Brent Geese arriving from the east. Something black and white scuds through the bottom of my scope view. Don't think it was an auk. Wasn't the white in the wrong places? Quick, swing scope left. Must get ahead of it. Here it comes. Argh, gone behind a wave. Definitely not an auk. It's got a long neck. And there's white in the wing. Don't think it's a merg. Heading west fast now. Need to get on it again. Before the shelter wall blocks my view. There. Argh. There. Yes! Two white triangles. Dirty head and neck. That'll probably be my only one of the year. Always a hard-won bird. A birder's bird they say. Definitely bird of the day.

The sun's out now, last of the squalls long gone. It's still windy but with the clearing horizon everything's moved further out. Even the Gannets are hard to see now. Packing up and walking down the main street back to the car, passing be-shorted families. They got ice creams, but I got Red-necked Grebe.

CHANGING BOCC STATUS 1–2–3–4

RED-LIST CRITERIA APPLICABLE

- IUCN Globally Threatened
- Historical breeding population decline
- Breeding population decline
- Non-breeding population decline
- Breeding range decline
- Non-breeding range decline

WORDS – SIMON GILLINGS | **ART** – RICHARD JOHNSON

R. Johnson '19.

13

Slavonian Grebe

Podiceps auritus

CHANGING BOCC STATUS 1–2–3–4

RED-LIST CRITERIA APPLICABLE

- IUCN Globally Threatened
- Historical breeding population decline
- Breeding population decline
- Non-breeding population decline
- Breeding range decline
- Non-breeding range decline

Undergoing a Cinderella-like transformation each spring, the Slavonian Grebe moults out of its dowdy winter attire, becoming one of our most spectacular breeding birds.

The neck and flanks are a luminous chestnut brown, contrasting with the matte black back and head. Both sexes sport flared, backswept golden ear tufts reminiscent of Hermes's winged helmet. These distinctive plumes give rise to the North American name, Horned Grebe, while folk names such as 'pink-eyed diver', 'devil-diver', 'hell-diver', and 'water witch', can be attributed to the startling ruby-red eyes. In Gaelic they are known as 'gobhlachan or-chlusach' (forked/sitting astride with gold ears), or 'gobhlachan mara' (forked/sitting astride the sea). These names make reference to the way in which they splay their legs to the side when swimming, using their large, lobed feet as both paddle and rudder. Their legs are set far back on their body, making them ungainly on land, but they are superlative swimmers, powering through the water in pursuit of fish and aquatic invertebrates.

The first breeding pair nested in Inverness-shire in 1908. Numbers increased slowly, peaking at around 80 pairs in the early 1990s, but the breeding population has declined considerably since then, with just 30 pairs remaining in their Highland stronghold. Half of these birds nest on the willow-flanked, sedge-fringed Loch Ruthven. Visit early in the season and you may be lucky enough to witness their balletic courtship display. Pairs head shake and bob-preen before swimming rapidly towards each other, rearing up breast-to-breast, and proffering love tokens of weed in their bills. Clutches of up to five eggs are laid on a floating platform of reeds and rotting vegetation, and from June the humbug-striped hatchlings can be spotted hitching rides on their parents' backs. Eggs, chicks and adults are vulnerable to predation, and nests can fail due to flooding; Slavonian Grebes are a climate-sensitive species and breeding success has likely been impacted by the increasingly warm, wet Scottish weather.

In autumn, Slavonian Grebes migrate to the UK's coastal bays and estuaries, where they can be spotted pitching forwards in rolling dives, water droplets beading off their feathers as they pop back up to the surface to swallow their prey. With the arrival of visitors from Scandinavia and Iceland numbers swell to over a thousand birds, but this overwintering population is also in decline.

WORDS – CLAIRE STARES | **ART –** ATM STREET ART

White-tailed Eagle

Haliaeetus albicilla

As it glides on its immense wings, a White-tailed Eagle stares intently at the coastal waters below. Before long it dives, throws its huge talons forward, and snatches a fish, with awe-inspiring ease. It departs with its catch as quickly as it appeared, an extraordinary blend of power and grace, that makes this – the world's fourth largest eagle – surely the most spectacular sight any birdwatcher can experience in the United Kingdom.

Like many birds of prey, the White-tailed Eagle has suffered greatly at the hands of humans. It was once widespread across the whole of the UK, ranging from the estuaries of the south coast to the wilds of the Hebrides. Evidence suggests the population may have peaked at 1,000–1,400 pairs in 500 CE but, as the centuries progressed, persecution decimated numbers. By the early 20th century it had been extirpated from the whole of the UK.

Fortunately, more enlightened thinking eventually came to the fore, and pioneering attempts were made to reintroduce White-tailed Eagles to Scotland in 1959 and 1968. Though unsuccessful, these efforts set an important precedent. Over the course of two decades, beginning in 1975, juvenile eagles from Norway were released on the Isle of Rum in the Hebrides and later at Loch Maree in Wester Ross. The first pair bred successfully in 1985 and there are now in excess of 130 pairs distributed across much of the north and west of Scotland. A further release of juvenile eagles in Fife has facilitated a further expansion to the east.

People now travel hundreds of miles to enjoy watching White-tailed Eagles in landscapes as majestic as the bird. On the Isle of Mull alone, eagle watchers are estimated to contribute more than £5 million to the local economy each year. The species has become synonymous with remote, wild places, but in continental Europe it prospers in the lowlands, close to people. In view of this, efforts are underway to reintroduce White-tailed Eagles in southern England, through a project based on the Isle of Wight. Significantly, there are now enough young eagles in Scotland for chicks to be translocated south.

Reintroducing the White-tailed Eagle to the Solent and surrounding estuaries, where it has been absent for more than two centuries, will not only reinstate an integral part of the local ecosystem, but also demonstrate how we can restore nature with positive action. Furthermore, it will enable many thousands more people to marvel at the sight of this most iconic of birds.

WORDS – TIM MACKRILL | **ART –** KEITH BROCKIE

CHANGING BOCC STATUS 1–2–3–4

RED-LIST CRITERIA APPLICABLE

- IUCN Globally Threatened
- Historical breeding population decline
- Breeding population decline
- Non-breeding population decline
- Breeding range decline
- Non-breeding range decline

adult ♀ sea eagle

L. Frisa, Isle of Mull

AM – 30th November 2003

sunning with wings held out and ruffled feathers blowing in the wind

Hen Harrier

Circus cyaneus

CHANGING BOCC STATUS 1–2–3–4

RED-LIST CRITERIA APPLICABLE

- IUCN Globally Threatened
- Historical breeding population decline
- Breeding population decline
- Non-breeding population decline
- Breeding range decline
- Non-breeding range decline

I have a lifelong love affair with Hen Harriers that dates back to my childhood. I grew up in mid-Wales, surrounded by the heather-clad Berwyn moorlands with its rare birds, such as Black Grouse, Golden Plover and Merlin.

The holy grail, however, was the Hen Harrier, and in particular the beautiful ghost-like male. During the 1970s these were incredibly scarce birds in the Welsh uplands, and a distant glimpse of a hunting bird was a memorable day. All of this changed one evening in late spring 1974 when, aged 11, I sat amongst some deep heather and watched transfixed as a male Hen Harrier passed a vole to a female that he had called off the nest. To this day, it remains the most memorable wildlife experience of my life; I still remember every second of that encounter as if it happened only yesterday.

Little did I know that this bird was to play a key role in my life. Every spring since that initial encounter I have wandered back up onto those moors to monitor 'my' birds. For 15 years, it was a privilege to monitor these most elegant of all our birds of prey in a professional capacity, working for the RSPB. Even with a busy spring filming schedule I have never failed to return to the Welsh hills for my Hen Harrier fix.

In Wales, this species is doing quite well. Some 40–60 pairs breed most years and apart from one north Wales moor, persecution appears to be largely absent. On driven grouse moors in northern England and parts of Scotland, however, Hen Harriers are shot and trapped in their hundreds each year. This is not an exaggeration; English moors should support more than 300 breeding pairs of Hen Harriers. Just six years ago, not a single pair nested successfully in England and in 2019 just a handful of pairs reared young. Such heavy levels of persecution were the norm in Victorian times, when the species was all but exterminated from mainland Britain, but this persecution is still going on today.

Moorland owners and their gamekeepers detest this bird because it feeds, amongst other things, on Red Grouse and it is said that the presence of a hunting harrier can adversely affect a day's shooting. Grouse moors are owned and managed by the elite for the elite and if driven grouse shooting is sustained by illegal persecution, then it has no place in modern society. I find it incredibly sad that a wider audience is robbed of an opportunity to enjoy such a beautiful bird because of the actions of a blinkered few. To watch a Hen Harrier quartering the moors is to witness aerial mastery in its most subtle form, and surely few spectacles in the bird world can match a male Hen Harrier 'skydancing' over its territory in early spring.

WORDS – IOLO WILLIAMS | **ART –** JANE SMITH

A/P

16 Corncrake

Crex crex

CHANGING BOCC STATUS 1–2–3–4

RED-LIST CRITERIA APPLICABLE

- IUCN Globally Threatened
- Historical breeding population decline
- Breeding population decline
- Non-breeding population decline
- Breeding range decline
- Non-breeding range decline

The evening was still, breath held, rhythmic frothing of reeds, pink summer sky. My weight was on the tarmac of the silent road and I stood, upright and waiting. Could I dare to hope, that the airspace could crackle with a 'crexing'?

The insidious decline of what once was heard in every field, is a heart-breaking travesty and a reflection of the charging of modernity, agricultural growth and of a world that is spinning recklessly out of control. Now, there are mostly lone males yearning into emptiness, calling all night for a mate.

I hear a different rush in the reeds, barely audible, and envision padding feet, slinking. A momentary twinkling of Twite and Linnet is stubbed to silence, as suddenly they are drowned out. A male Corncrake, croaking into the wilderness. I see faintly, the palette of reeds and plumage mixed together, and a neck craned to the sky, beak wide open, a stream of desperation.

The older people I talk to tell what seem like tall tales of abundance, and of the hollow left by emptiness and decimation. Each year I witness fields emptied for silage multiple times a summer, heftily moved by pounding blades; these secretive, ground nesting landrails don't stand a chance. Islands have the right idea, less intensive land use, more Corncrakes. My mum and dad heard the Corncrake in 1997, a sound my mum had heard frequently in childhood. A male calling strong, accompanied by a female in full sight, on their honeymoon in Iona. Tory, Inishbofin, the Hebrides all cradle a delicate and fragile breeding population.

My heart is instantly buoyed by the sight and sound of it, before the crashing realisation that it flew all the way from sub-Saharan Africa to croon all night, for many weeks, with no sign of a mate. A tear slithers out and I feel a hand on my shoulder, my dad squeezes my hand. Will my generation ever live to see the abundance that he enjoyed as a boy? As long as I live, I will dedicate my life to act in the hope that we can restore our natural world, our meadows, that these ghostly cries will be answered and balance restored. We walk away reverently, knowing the sad magnitude of what we have heard, but a little hope fluttered as we purposefully moved onwards.

WORDS – DARA MCANULTY | **ART –** ROBERT VAUGHAN

17

Lapwing

Vanellus vanellus

CHANGING BoCC STATUS 1–2–3–4

RED-LIST CRITERIA APPLICABLE
- IUCN Globally Threatened
- Historical breeding population decline
- Breeding population decline
- Non-breeding population decline
- Breeding range decline
- Non-breeding range decline

It's the crest that does it for me – that flicked nib stroke, the artist's afterthought.

It's the colouring that does it too. Black bib; white belly leaking into the wingpits; orange undercarriage, half hidden; the back – black at first glance, revealing its true colours in good light – dark green with subtle purple iridescence.

It's the shape of their wings – broad, rounded at the tip – reminiscent of wide-handled table tennis bats, their lazy flaps disguising enviable grace and control.

It's the name, for years associated in my mind with the lapping of their wings, but apparently derived from the old English for 'crested bird'; and all the folk names too, 'peewit' the most obvious and famous.

It's the voice, the source of that 'peewit' and all its variants, the throaty swoops and slides bringing to mind – mine, at least – the 1980s video game Galaxian.

It's the display flight, those languorous laps producing apparently effortless swoops and jinks and tumbles and glides and rolls – intended to catch the eye of a potential mate, but mesmerising to humans too. A flamboyant and brilliant spectacle of aerobatics, full of improvised flourishes and curlicues, the casual understatement of the landing – a Clooney-esque "Hello ladies" – capping the display. All available to the observer entirely free of charge.

It's the way they stand on the scrape, stolid in the teeth of driving rain, somehow – and I know this is fanciful, but can we not occasionally yield to the temptation of mild anthropomorphism? – exuding an aura of pluckiness absent in other birds.

But what really does it, the thing that makes me want to drink in every last sighting of them, is the memory, clean and crisp and etched into my brain from across four decades, of flocks of Lapwings billowing up in the wake of tractors in the fields around our village, their abundance taken for granted, their place in the fabric of our countryside unquestioned. The fields are a golf course now; the Lapwings not completely gone, but much denuded, victims of modern life.

So when I see a Lapwing, a 'peewit', a 'green plover', a 'tieve's nacket', a 'toppyup', a 'teeick' – call it what you will – I stay a while and savour it, even when all there is to savour is a distant blob, that wispy crest standing to attention, reminding me of days long gone.

WORDS – LEV PARIKIAN | **ART –** JOHN LLOYD

18

Ringed Plover

Charadrius hiaticula

They gather at high tide like shoppers waiting for a bus: all facing the same direction, and all staring into the distance. For Ringed Plovers, as with all waders, this is a hiatus in their busy lives, when for an hour or two they are unable to feed. Yet they cannot afford to lose concentration: at any moment a Peregrine or Merlin could swoop down and make a kill.

When the tide begins to fall, areas of food-rich mud start to appear, and the birds disperse from the roost. Like other members of their family, Ringed Plovers are surface feeders: using that short, stubby bill to pick up invertebrates from the surface of the mud. They feed methodically, taking a couple of steps forward, bending down to grab an item of food, and then moving on.

As with so many other birds, this is all about energy. During the crucial period when the mud is exposed, they must get as much food as they can; for it is September, and they have stopped off to refuel on the Somerset coast, on their long journey south.

Ringed Plovers are one of those birds I used to take for granted. They are not particularly rare, and have a rather chunky appearance, as if they need to eat less and do more exercise. For me, I confess that the Little Ringed Plover has always been more of a favourite. That is not just because of their slim and elegant pose, set off by the narrow yellow eye-ring, but also because they first nested in Britain on gravel pits near my childhood home, in suburban west London.

Yet my view of the Ringed Plover changed a few years ago, when I visited Iceland at the height of summer. As we walked along a beach, we came across a bird a few metres in front of us, which immediately began to hold out her wing, and stagger like a late-night drunk across the shingle. I immediately realised that this was what ornithologists call the 'distraction display'; and that she was feigning injury, in order to lure me and my companions away from her eggs or chicks.

This is a high-risk strategy: a predator may not be fooled, or the adult Plover may allow it to get too close, and be seized itself. For me, though, it summed up the extraordinary way that bird behaviour evolves to give a better chance of survival. If she succeeded, this little wader and her chicks would then have flown all the way to North Africa, to spend the winter there. Knowing that made the experience even more special.

CHANGING BoCC STATUS 1–2–3–4

RED-LIST CRITERIA APPLICABLE

- IUCN Globally Threatened
- Historical breeding population decline
- Breeding population decline
- Non-breeding population decline
- Breeding range decline
- Non-breeding range decline

WORDS – STEPHEN MOSS | **ART –** RACHEL C. TAYLOR

19

Dotterel

Charadrius morinellus

Dotterel, oh Dotterel. When will I see you? One day. One day, when you're not even on my mind. When I'm just ambling. High up on a Scottish mountaintop, pure sun – but no swelterer – plenty of breeze, sway in the air just right. Pub meal to look forward to in the evening. Solo. Peace.

No big ideas today. Just percolating. Walking the day, walking the day. Free on the plateaux. Timeless, out of time in time.

Then – hang on.

What was that? Movement? Something behind that tuft of grass ... a quick runner ... all goes still again. Did I dream it? Was it a Rabbit?

Pause. Then. Okay okay. There's something there again. And this ain't no Curlew. This ain't no Redshank either.

Then the thought lands. Could it be you? I mean – this high up ... who else could it be?

Heart going b-boom. There it is now, out in the open, fully. Hands shaking slightly. Binoculars up. Oh sweet Bonanza! Dotterel, it really is! It really is you! Finally!

Run run run. Still. Still still. Run run. Still. Run Run Run. Still again. On you go. Just like I imagined. You look like you know something I don't. Alert, but you're not troubled. Just switched on. There's something ancient about you. You've got allure, Dotterel. You always have had.

Ever since I saw you on the telly. Tony Soper. I was six, maybe eight. What is it about you that's always had me? Is it the eye-stripe? An eye-stripe usually helps. But no ... do you know what it is, Dotterel? I have it now. It's your rufous-ness, Dotterel. Your very rufous-ness. Your full-blown, summer plumage, puffed up belly of rufous-ness.

What is it with that colour you waders wear in summer? It reels me in. It's an illogical colour. It has no place on mudflats or mountains. And yet there it is. A colour that has answers. A colour that's seen things. Basic and deep.

Yeah, that's how I want to meet you, Dotterel.

Not blown in on an October Norfolk playing field, all drab and befuddled, press pack of birders onto you, shutters snapping rapid style. That's not you.

Nah. I want you in the mountains. Summer breeze. At home. Doing your thing.

So don't go disappearing on us, okay?

We've a moment to have.

CHANGING BOCC STATUS 1–2–3–4

RED-LIST CRITERIA APPLICABLE
- IUCN Globally Threatened
- Historical breeding population decline
- Breeding population decline
- Non-breeding population decline
- Breeding range decline
- Non-breeding range decline

WORDS – FYFE DANGERFIELD | **ART –** DAN BRADBURY

20 Whimbrel

Numenius phaeopus

I only know the Whimbrel passing through. On Scolt Head Island, on the North Norfolk coast in July, the Whimbrel sounds a melancholy note as it flies low over the purple-swathed salt marsh. Melancholy is the Whimbrel's natural sound, plaintive and liquid, like its similar looking and much better known big sibling, the Eurasian Curlew. But it is also melancholy because this elegant wader is already heading to overwinter in West Africa, and summer is on the turn.

At Wells-next-the-Sea in spring, the Whimbrel stands in ankle-deep water at low tide, pecking and prospecting between the trickle and dazzle. It's refuelling again, picking tiny molluscs and invisible shrimps from between rounded flints, before heading further north to breed.

Most of us, I think, only know the Whimbrel in passing. There are only eight species of curlew in the world and the Whimbrel is one of two found in Britain. We know all about the travails of 'our' Curlew, which is much bigger, and is more conspicuous in our culture too. But the trim, curlew-coloured Whimbrel, possessing a beak that curves downwards like the Curlew – but is much shorter, is a more modest presence in our land. It breeds in small numbers on Shetland, Orkney and in the far north of Scotland, and makes a fleeting passage through the rest of Britain in unobtrusive small flocks, emitting its seven-note call as it goes.

The Whimbrel's old name is the 'Seven Whistler'. According to legend, if you hear seven Whimbrel pass over at night, death will follow. In 1862, locals in Hartley, Northumberland, claimed they heard the seven whistlers the night before a pumping engine fell down a coal mine, trapping and killing 204 miners below ground. Twelve years later, miners refused to go to work in Bedworth, near Coventry, because local people had heard the 'Seven Whistlers' passing overhead the previous night.

Today, in the Anthropocene, the death of species other than our own is writ large. How often do Whimbrels pass overhead nowadays? Unseen and unheard, their calls mean nothing to most of us.

Is the Whimbrel a species that is passing through? Only time will tell. But the more we pay this unassuming bird the attention it deserves, the more chance it has got of finding a way through the extinction crisis.

CHANGING BOCC STATUS 1–2–3–4

RED-LIST CRITERIA APPLICABLE
- IUCN Globally Threatened
- Historical breeding population decline
- Breeding population decline
- Non-breeding population decline
- Breeding range decline
- Non-breeding range decline

WORDS – PATRICK BARKHAM | **ART –** MARCO BRODDE

21 Curlew

Numenius arquata

If I was asked to think of a colloquial name for Curlews, I would call them mud-gluggers. They are the ultimate sticky beaks, putting their nose into the hidden world of gloop and creating mayhem. Crabs, worms and molluscs have much to fear, but the rest of us just see a lanky-legged, long-nosed wild poet that wanders where we cannot tread and that cries and bubbles across the landscape. Perhaps it is because they make me smile and wonder in equal measure that I love them so much; and the fact they are achingly vulnerable in a world that is battling to hold onto loveliness.

It is when they soar in fresh air, singing their rising, curling song, wrapping a whole host of meanings into a swirl of notes, that I feel I have come home. Perhaps I was a Curlew in a previous life and their songs touch some ancestral memory that now lies deep within a 21st century human soul. Maybe I strutted across primaeval marshes as cold winter winds blew, or nestled into warm grass in the summer, with the thrum of insects all around. Or maybe I'm just edging into Pseuds Corner and should step back into the reality of today and simply accept that Curlews are birds that, for some reason, just do it for me.

We all need them, these totem creatures. Perhaps the more resolutely scientific don't like to think of nature in these terms, but I for sure need a spirit guide to help me navigate the confusing and labyrinthine world of conservation. Look at the UK through Curlew eyes and the complexity surrounding really knotty, intense issues (farming, wetland conservation, upland management, afforestation, predator control, climate change…) find a clearer focus. Without them I would founder in these turbulent seas, unable to find a holdfast. Curlews are my rock and my lighthouse as I search for answers to deeply troubling questions about humanity's role on Planet Earth.

It is a big burden to place on the feathery shoulders of a wading bird, but without them, and all the other creatures of wild and wet places, I know I would have sunk beneath the waves a long time ago. They keep me focussed. I would weep for a thousand years if Curlews went extinct as a breeding bird in Britain. I will continue to try to make sure that doesn't happen on my watch.

CHANGING BOCC STATUS 1–2–3–4

RED-LIST CRITERIA APPLICABLE
- IUCN Globally Threatened
- Historical breeding population decline
- Breeding population decline
- Non-breeding population decline
- Breeding range decline
- Non-breeding range decline

WORDS – MARY COLWELL | **ART –** KERRIE ANN GARDNER

KG

Black-tailed Godwit

Limosa limosa

A glimpse of terracotta is obscured by ripples of grass, dipping gently in the breeze. Then she appears, gliding, effortless through the vegetation. Moving with purpose, alert to the ever-present dangers. She turns her head and her long bill becomes visible against the light, the perfect adaptation for her environment, and yet the unintended elegance is inescapable. I hear the buzz of insects and can smell the freshness of the marsh. Alive and simultaneously still, this is a special place, and home to a very special bird.

Nearby the male stands on careful watch. He has a job to do. Both have travelled thousands of miles from the wetlands of West Africa and southern Europe to reunite in this same place. He creates several shallow nest scrapes in the grass for her to inspect. She will lay four perfectly camouflaged, olive-coloured eggs, which are incubated in turn by the parents; the resulting chicks a mottled mix of caramel tones, designed for hiding in the grass. But for a ground-nesting bird, dangers from predators and flooding may lie in wait.

It is the breeding population of the *limosa* subspecies, found in perilously small numbers in the Cambridgeshire and Norfolk fens which affords the Black-tailed Godwit its Red-listed status. In the 1800s Black-tailed Godwits were lost as a breeding species as a result of the large-scale drainage of wetland habitat. They recolonised in the 1930–40s, at a time when the population in mainland Europe was increasing, but the species now finds itself back on the brink of extinction. Conservationists from the RSPB and WWT are bringing fresh hope to the species. Collecting eggs, rearing and releasing birds into areas of grassland that have been created especially for them – a technique known as headstarting. The early signs are encouraging. These godwits, reared by people, have migrated thousands of miles returning a stone's throw away from where they were released and have bred successfully. Three years in, released birds now make up a quarter of this fragile population. Perhaps for the Black-tailed Godwits, the odds may be finally turning in their favour.

In a moment they are gone, retreating into the cover of the grass. I hope they will safely raise their chicks and return next year. A fleeting encounter is enough; I am happy knowing they are there.

CHANGING BOCC STATUS 1–2–3–4

RED-LIST CRITERIA APPLICABLE

- IUCN Globally Threatened
- Non-breeding population decline
- Historical breeding population decline
- Breeding range decline
- Breeding population decline
- Non-breeding range decline

WORDS – HANNAH WARD | **ART –** ED KEEBLE

Ed Keeble

23 Ruff

Calidris pugnax

"How are you feeling?" "Rough!" This phrase often goes through my head as I train my scope on the nearest Ruff. They are odd birds, with a spectacular and gaudy lekking display where males joust for the attention of the ladies – an event not readily seen in the UK with its tiny and declining breeding population. They usually appear either with scrappy, oddly painted plumage after the breeding season, or in their variable, pale winter garb. A bad hair day, or a rather gormless expression, so sometimes I think they do look a bit rough – the morning after the night before.

For me Ruff is a harbinger of autumn. Birders have a strange affinity for rushing headlong into autumn when most families are still at the beach. My records on the BTO survey BirdTrack tell me that I have seen Ruff in every month of the year, and that it is early August when their numbers really build up on the North Norfolk coast. Sitting on the bank at Titchwell with the evening sun behind lighting up the freshmarsh beautifully is, for me, seeing Ruffs at their best. Their variety of plumage is astonishing, and confusing for the beginner birder. I am often asked to help decipher these strange waders.

They look a bit inelegant – a small head for a decently sized bird, a halting gait, and that oddly vacant face. Males are much larger than females, so describing to someone that these birds of very different sizes in front of us are the same species is the first obstacle. Then plumage variability – most have greyish upperparts with pale feather edges giving a scalloped look, whiteish underparts, and a pale face. But not all are like this: some birds can still retain striking black and gold vermiculations from summer dress, and even untidy remnants of that Elizabethan fluff around their neck that give the bird its name. What's more, these feathers can be either stark white, black or rufous – yep, black and white and red all over. Still confused? Even the best of birders can sometimes do a double take before resting on the identification of a Ruff, albeit an odd one.

However, as autumn advances, Ruffs are rescued in the looks department by their youngsters. Fresh, gingery feathered arrivals, neatly scalloped with pale edges, a dark eye in a warm brown face and a neat black bill – a quintessential autumn wader.

CHANGING BOCC STATUS 1–2–3–4

RED-LIST CRITERIA APPLICABLE
- IUCN Globally Threatened
- Historical breeding population decline
- Breeding population decline
- Non-breeding population decline
- Breeding range decline
- Non-breeding range decline

WORDS – ANDY CLEMENTS | **ART –** LIZ TOOLE

liz Toole

Red-necked Phalarope

Phalaropus lobatus

The morning mist clung close to the ground, partially hiding the softly undulating, marshy landscape of Fetlar. A small bird fluttered into view and dropped onto the surface of the dark grey pool. The Red-necked Phalarope paddled along, snatching flies from the water in fast, jerky movements, droplets dripping from its slender beak. It was so absorbed that it swam to within a few feet of me, completely unperturbed. Other little birds – chirruping to each other – soon joined it, turning, lunging, spinning as they fed. They were all female, with white throats and orange-red necks, neat little white spots above their eyes, and wavy golden stripes down their grey backs.

Somewhere in the long grass nearby were the males. In a reversal of the usual parenting roles, the male Red-necked Phalarope – plainer, paler and browner than the female – incubates the clutch of four eggs and raises the young by himself. The females court and mate, often with more than one male, when the birds return in mid- to late-May. But it's a short summer – the females leave in late-July, followed by the males and young.

Most of us only get to see these dainty waders in their duller brown, grey and white plumage as they stop along our coasts on migration in spring and autumn. In spite of their small size (adults are about 18 cm long and weigh 30–40 g), Red-necked Phalaropes spend much of their lives on the oceans. It had been thought that British birds, as with Scandinavian Red-necked Phalaropes, migrate south to winter in the Arabian Sea. But, in 2013, researchers found that a Shetland male had travelled across the Atlantic, all the way to the Pacific, and stayed in plankton-rich waters near Ecuador and the Galapagos Islands, before returning in spring – a round trip of 26,000 km.

In northern Scotland, the Red-necked Phalarope is on the southern edge of its breeding range, with Shetland – especially Fetlar – its stronghold in the UK. Thanks to conservation work, the population has increased from just a handful of breeding males to 60 across Shetland in 2015, as well as record numbers at key sites elsewhere in Scotland.

But it's feared that climate change will soon affect the Red-necked Phalaropes' breeding habitat, primarily in the Arctic, making it largely unsuitable for them. For Shetland's precarious population, however, the condition of their wintering areas in the Pacific Ocean may be just as important to the future of these pretty little birds.

CHANGING BOCC STATUS 1–2–3–4

RED-LIST CRITERIA APPLICABLE

- IUCN Globally Threatened
- Historical breeding population decline
- Breeding population decline
- Non-breeding population decline
- Breeding range decline
- Non-breeding range decline

WORDS – ROB YARHAM | **ART –** DARREN REES

Darren Rees

Woodcock

Scolopax rusticola

CHANGING BOCC STATUS 1-2-3-4

RED-LIST CRITERIA APPLICABLE

- IUCN Globally Threatened
- Historical breeding population decline
- Breeding population decline
- Non-breeding population decline
- Breeding range decline
- Non-breeding range decline

The Woodcock is inseparable from its environment. A prober of damp woodland, its cryptic camouflage blends bands and bars of foxed chestnuts, mollusc browns and heartwood creams, marbled black and ash greys; rust, cola.

Woodcock shares the same crepuscular puppetry of Nightjar. Its spring dusk 'roding' flights are arresting; a slow, beating-the-bounds along invisible roads at tree top height. In open air theatre clearings, under a lamplight moon, it performs, silhouetted, in the round, vocalising a froggy "*ort, ort, ort*", and a pig-squeal. Occasionally, the flight-paths of patrolling males overlap in the shallowest of venn diagrams, when birds glance around each other.

The nest is a feathered scrape on the ground. Hen Woodcock are believed to carry their chicks from danger in their feet, or pressed between legs and body. But the migration myth of Goldcrests 'piloting' Woodcock over the North Sea, remains just that. Woodcock flight seems workmanlike, with intent only to land. Disturbed, it appears as loose ground come adrift, long bill pointed down; a balancing needle or divining rod, angled so that even in flight it has not lost contact with the earth.

Drayton, Shakespeare and Milton used the bird as a metaphor for foolish love for its unwillingness to hop over objects. Simple, maze-like 'springes' were set to catch a bird easily led down a garden path or 'cockerode'. Our resident population (55,241 pairs) is boosted to 1.4 million individuals in winter, making journeys averaging 3,000 km from frozen Europe when they can no longer access food. They are still shot as game.

Feeding nightly, Woodcock gather like groups of Victorian philosophers, wings clasped behind backs, isolated in thought. They probe the earth with an extraordinarily long bill, exploratory core-drilling; taking the earth's temperature with the precision of a slow, sewing-machine needle, unthreading worms and snags of beetle from the fabric of the earth, sucking them up like spaghetti.

On hands and knees, I have got about as close as it's possible to get to a Woodcock. It sat like a wooden carving. An upturned boat of a body, a dumpy wood ark, a vessel of worms clinker-built with lines of owly feathers. Its large, intelligent eye, set high on its rounded, banded, umbrella-handle head, glinted like a tiny onyx. I saw the mobile bump at the end of its bill, move. Water oozed through stitch-holes made by it moments before, between my splayed fingers.

WORDS – NICOLA CHESTER | **ART –** JAMES O'NEILL

26 Arctic Skua

Stercorarius parasiticus

CHANGING BOCC STATUS 1–2–3–4

RED-LIST CRITERIA APPLICABLE

- IUCN Globally Threatened
- Historical breeding population decline
- Breeding population decline
- Non-breeding population decline
- Breeding range decline
- Non-breeding range decline

A fleeting glimpse at an autumnal sea-watch might be the only dose of Arctic Skua most birders get for the year. If you really want to see these birds close up, you need to venture to the rugged moors and heaths of the northernmost parts of the British Isles: calling, chasing and tumbling above their breeding grounds, surrounded by stunning landscapes – the very best way to see Arctic Skuas.

These are marauders of the sea and sky, true pirates, pillaging food from other seabirds in an act of thievery known as kleptoparasitism. However, a reduction in sand eel stocks, a consequence of fishing activities and climate change, along with competition on the breeding grounds from their bigger cousins Great Skuas, are thought to be contributing to the decline of this otherwise wily pirate.

Arctic Skuas have been tracked using GPS and geolocator tags in an attempt to better understand the declines; these allow us to follow birds throughout their annual cycle. As a fieldworker, you can't help but feel connected to the lives of individual birds, especially when they are physically connecting with you so regularly! Arctic Skuas dive-bomb anyone (human, bird or mammal) who dares to approach their precious eggs or chicks, and they soon learn who the fieldworkers are, paying them 'special attention'!

Despite this, fieldwork throws up those special moments. One morning, visibility poor and wet fog blanketing Fair Isle, the skuas unexpectedly pierced the silent, heavy air with calls, before slicing through the dense fog with sudden and close appearances, bombing around our heads and chasing one another! A mad half hour passed before this wild game ended as abruptly as it had started, and they all settled back into the fog to continue the grown-up business of incubation. A truly thrilling experience!

The tracking project is now in a post-fieldwork stage but it appears foraging trip-length plays an important role in breeding success; Fair Isle birds travel as far south as Fraserburgh, whilst those on Rousay stay closer to home. Whilst both populations are declining, breeding productivity appears to be better on Rousay than Fair Isle.

These Arctic Skuas are struggling, with nesting attempts abandoned or birds eating their own eggs, usually after a long fruitless foraging trip by one of the pair. Our research is ongoing, but preliminary results are encouraging. If we can identify problems, then solutions may be found to reverse the fortunes of this enigmatic and wonderful bird before we lose it from our shores altogether.

WORDS – SARAH HARRIS | **ART –** LEO DU FEU

Leo duFeu

27

Puffin

Fratercula arctica

CHANGING BOCC STATUS 1–2–3–4

RED-LIST CRITERIA APPLICABLE

- IUCN Globally Threatened
- Historical breeding population decline
- Breeding population decline
- Non-breeding population decline
- Breeding range decline
- Non-breeding range decline

All my life – or at least every summer since I was eight years old – I have loved to sit and watch the great wheels of Puffins on the Shiant Isles in the Outer Hebrides. My father took me there when I was a boy and by my teens I was addicted to the place: wildness, beauty, boats, caves, lobsters, a huge scale of undiminished life.

And of course the birds: the air in summer, all day and on into the evening, was filled with the whirr of wings and then, deep into the night, with the calls and grumbles of the giant colonies, so that in a calm out in the bay between the islands, the sounds were those of a hospital ward, the patients shuffling in their beds; distant coughing, now and then a deeper groan, a mass of life at rest.

But the Puffin wheel was the thing. Morning and evening in the breeding season, their numbers growing and the wheels thickening as the weeks go by, the Puffins circle above their nesting slopes, upwind over the colony itself, downwind a hundred yards or so offshore.

If the wind is strong, they fly into it almost at the same speed as they are blown back, and so the birds hang in front of you, sometimes no more than 10 feet away, busy, looking resolutely forward and then sideways to see what you are, their features not sleek as they are at rest but ruffled, troubled, with the look of boats working in a tideway, more real and mysteriously more serious, just as drivers' faces passed on the road are surprisingly intense and inward, than the neat, brushed creatures you meet standing at the colony.

It is a glimpse of the ocean bird, not on display but at work, the bird that dies in winter out in Atlantic storms, that goes 300 miles or more in search of food in a bad year for chicks it knows are hungry in the burrow, an animal whose life stands outside the cuteness in which we always want to envelop it.

It is a sight and a memory which makes me impatient with all the talk of Puffins as sweet little clowns. They are not toys, but superbly successful ocean predators, beauties, Ice Age survivors, their minds on an everlasting swing between island and sea, burrow and voyage. They just happen each summer to get dressed like Colonel Gadaffi.

WORDS – ADAM NICOLSON | **ART –** APITHANNY BOURNE

28

Roseate Tern

Sterna dougallii

CHANGING BOCC STATUS 1–2–3–4

RED-LIST CRITERIA APPLICABLE
- IUCN Globally Threatened
- Historical breeding population decline
- Breeding population decline
- Non-breeding population decline
- Breeding range decline
- Non-breeding range decline

At Mietkowski Lake near Wrocław, on 12 July 2013, there was an amazing sighting of Poland's first inland record of Roseate Tern. What makes this even more fantastic is that this bird was ringed. Pictures were taken, the 'special' ring was read as '93P3', and circulated via the Internet; within hours of it being found there was connection. I had ringed it on Coquet Island, Northumberland, as a chick in July 2010. What were the chances, and what was it doing there in the middle of the breeding season?

Back to 1992 when I was asked to help ring Roseate Terns, by RSPB, on Coquet Island; the population had, scarily, fallen to around 20 pairs. Although in world terms not a lot was known about breeding numbers, the nominate race *dougallii*, found in the Atlantic, was in 'free fall' – but why?

In those early days birds made their nests in simple scrapes, almost always near a Puffin nesting burrow, all around the island; nesting boxes and shingle terraces were ideas of futuristic fantasy. RSPB wardens worked hard to track down each nesting attempt by listening for the distinctive calls and watching carefully where birds settled. During my ringing visits we would walk the island looking for chicks, which had the sneaky habit of hiding in burrows. It was my 'labour of love' to shove an arm through Puffin latrines in the hope of finding 'that' missing chick.

Nesting boxes – an idea brought from North America via Rockabill – and shingle terraces proved to be the turning point for Coquet Island's Roseate Terns, by providing protection from the elements and from predators.

These new 'housing estates' have made life easier, not just for the Roseate Terns but also for us humans. Now each ringing expedition is relatively short, thereby reducing disturbance. Even after all of these years of ringing I still feel incredibly privileged to be working on 'Roseys'. Sitting within the colony ringing chicks, the thrill continues when I look along the rows to see those glowing 'pink breasts' of the adults, quick to return to sit confidingly on top of those nesting boxes.

So, hats off – or perhaps on, for protection against dive-bombing terns – to the dedicated work of numerous Coquet Island wardens who, over the years, have made a significant difference by helping the breeding population get on the road to recovery.

WORDS – TOM CADWALLENDER | **ART –** FIONA GOMEZ

Kittiwake

Rissa tridactyla

When I think of our gulls my mind turns to the Kittiwake. I don't think a lot of people would immediately think of this neat pelagic seabird but instead associate the word 'gull' with a nuisance Herring Gull in a city centre, after your chips. The Kittiwake isn't anything like this. While I have equal respect and admiration for our other gulls, the Kittiwake is what I would consider a true gull; a gull of the sea and a beautiful one at that.

The Kittiwake is a small, slender, elegant bird. They are highly pelagic outside the breeding season and as immatures, but during those few months they are on land they can be found on the narrow ledges of steep towering cliffs. Kittiwakes never fail to surprise me. Just when you think they couldn't nest in any more precarious a place you peer up to see a pair of dazzling white faces staring right back at you, as they nest unfazed on the steepest, most inaccessible ledge. I remember this moment very well while on a rather small dodgy inflatable boat being thrown around by the swell into Ramsey island's most hidden caves.

I associate the Kittiwake with windswept afternoons and sideways rain along the South Wales coast – my home. I guess I've been spoilt. While the vast majority of colonies in the UK are found in the north and west of Britain and Ireland, I am lucky enough to have access to a colony of Kittiwakes right on my doorstep on Skomer island. Many a day has been spent sat on a particularly crowded part of Skomer, called 'The Wick', watching the Kittiwakes on their nests, bringing back material like seaweed, mud or grass, heading out to sea to forage or the odd Peregrine causing a flurry amongst the colony. It is what kicked off my fascination with Kittiwakes. Sitting in the wind, clinging onto a warm flask of tea while listening to the distinctive "*Kitti-wayke*" call echoing across the cliff towards me.

There has been a long-term decline in numbers, the UK population falling by 50% since the mid-1980's. During the 19th century Kittiwake skins were prized by hunters because of their striking wing plumage. Some populations increased during the 20th century, yet today we again see them in decline. This time it is the anthropogenic effects on our climate, causing changes in the marine environment. Sand eel populations, a major food source, are collapsing due to warming oceans. Next spring I will be visiting Skomer once again, in excitement and anticipation of the return of the familiar sounds, sights and smells of a crowded cliff full of nesting Kittiwakes... but not without worry about how many of these birds will return.

CHANGING BOCC STATUS 1–2–3–4

RED-LIST CRITERIA APPLICABLE
- IUCN Globally Threatened
- Historical breeding population decline
- Breeding population decline
- Non-breeding population decline
- Breeding range decline
- Non-breeding range decline

WORDS – LIZZIE DALY | **ART –** DICK GILHESPY

Dick Gilhespy.

Herring Gull

Larus argentatus

CHANGING BOCC STATUS 1–2–3–4

RED-LIST CRITERIA APPLICABLE

- IUCN Globally Threatened
- Historical breeding population decline
- Breeding population decline
- Non-breeding population decline
- Breeding range decline
- Non-breeding range decline

Trash bird, dump gull, terror, menace. These are all words used to describe an icon of the British coast, the Herring Gull. With their familiar call, which nearly everyone knows (even if they call them 'seagulls'), few species have such a poor, and perhaps undeserved, reputation.

For many, the Herring Gull is a nuisance, pest, or threat, but in reality they are true marvels of evolution – highly adaptive, successful, and versatile. They also epitomise some of the great challenges we have in living with wildlife today.

With the advent of industrial fishing in the post-war years came an abundance of free food, in the form of fish or bait thrown overboard, and less-than-ideal waste management at rubbish tips, together fuelling a veritable boom in the Herring Gull population across Europe. Always opportunistic, Herring Gulls exploit a huge array of food sources, from intertidal mussels and foraged fish to fisheries discards, rubbish tip food waste, and food in bins. This adaptability has brought Herring Gulls into an increasing number of conflicts with people, with tabloid headlines and even members of Parliament warning us of seagulls as big as dogs attacking pensioners in seaside towns. But despite their apparent evolutionary success, Herring Gulls in the UK and Ireland are not faring well.

Peaking in the 1960s, Herring Gull populations fell by about 1% per year until 1985, then by 1.5% per year until 2000. From 2000–2013, numbers, particularly on the coasts, have dropped by 3% a year. Since the first census in the late 1960s, numbers have declined rapidly across Ireland, Scotland, England, and Wales, falling by half to two thirds and with ever more birds shifting into urban areas, which not only makes them more difficult to count, but also increases the chances of negative interactions with people. Between 2013 and 2018, more than 16,000 were authorised to be culled in England, deemed a threat to people, human health, or a nuisance.

With the Herring Gull, inaction around the declines often reflects the perception that they are 'too abundant' or that populations were 'artificially inflated' in the 1960s and 1970s, an argument that is not put forward for other species that are heavily reliant on humans for food. The challenge before us is how to best look after a declining species that is so readily brought into conflict with people, but it's clear the answer can't be the status quo.

WORDS – ALEX BOND | **ART –** CROW ARTIST

31

Turtle Dove

Streptopelia turtur

Dove Step has been a huge part of my life for over six years now. For the uninitiated, Dove Step entails my friends and I enduring for Turtle Doves, by undertaking arduous journeys to raise both awareness and funds for Operation Turtle Dove. To date, we have raised over £19,000 and endured over 1,930 miles for Turtle Doves, across three journeys and just 57 Dove Step days.

Dove Step has drawn a line from the north-east of England to Tarifa in southern Spain, via a 300 mile walk connecting the Saltholme and Lakenheath Fen RSPB reserves, Channel distance sea kayak, 700 mile cycle/walk the length of France and the last journey – a complete walk of Spain. The last journey comprised a 704.5 mile walk undertaken in just 28 days and with no rest days – connecting Tarifa beach in the south and Gijon in northern Spain, a complete on-foot crossing of the entire country, cumulating in the crossing of the mighty Picos de Europa. Our efforts aimed to mimic the twice annual migratory route of our UK Turtle Doves.

My passion for Turtle Doves stems from my appreciation and enjoyment in watching the birds themselves and the fact that they are, for me, a flagship species. They are a flagship for all Afro-European migrants, all Red-listed species, for our farmland birds here in the UK and all species in decline. Dove Step is a focal point for my frustration and sometimes anger at the current lack of political and social care for our natural world. Dove Step acts as a vent, a catharsis – I can read yet another bleak headline or learn of yet another wildlife crime and channel that emotion into something useful. My training, writing, public speaking or, of course, the execution of another Dove Step journey, all allow me to go beyond motivation, which may be superficial and applied in the lead-up to a given race or event. I am driven, almost daily, for Turtle Doves and for our Red-listed birds.

We started our preparation for the first Dove Step journey, a 300 mile walk here in the UK, back in 2013 and over the course of six years and literally thousands of miles, I have changed physically and also added Turtle Dove themed tattoos to my arms, blending my love of both heavy metal and this treasured species.

Don't forget Turtle Doves and please don't forget Dove Step.

CHANGING BOCC STATUS 1–2–3–4

RED-LIST CRITERIA APPLICABLE
- IUCN Globally Threatened
- Historical breeding population decline
- Breeding population decline
- Non-breeding population decline
- Breeding range decline
- Non-breeding range decline

WORDS – JONNY RANKIN | **ART –** MATT SEWELL

Cuckoo

Cuculus canorus

CHANGING BOCC STATUS 1–2–3–4

RED-LIST CRITERIA APPLICABLE

- IUCN Globally Threatened
- Historical breeding population decline
- Breeding population decline
- Non-breeding population decline
- Breeding range decline
- Non-breeding range decline

It's April and a Chiffchaff sings loudly from an Ash tree as I walk into the wood. Apple blossom is opening and the sun has a gentle warmth. The birdsong in the wood is a cacophony, a heady jumble of tweets from Blackcap, Wren, Chaffinch, Song Thrush and others so numerous I can't distinguish them.

As I reach a clearing in the wood the volume of birdsong drops to a sort of melodic interference, a background flurry of notes and I can make out individual songs: the cackle of a Green Woodpecker, the see-sawing tune of a Great Tit. Then I hear another bird, ghostly at first and barely audible. At first I assume it's a Woodpigeon, but the rhythm is different. The lower note is being repeated, like a quiet alarm. As the direction of the wind shifts I catch the upper note, repeated, like the lower, to create that elusive sound that has been associated with impending summer for tens of thousands of years: a Cuckoo.

I'm filled with a tumbling mixture of feelings. This simple, two-note song evokes childhood memories of days out in North Wales, of being enchanted by the green of wild places. I feel a pang of empathy for the unfortunate chicks that will be shoved out of fenland nests by the children of the bird I can hear; the Cuckoo is the cheat, the ornithological freeloader and its call heralds furtive bird crimes in hedgerows and among tufts of reed. Finally I feel a bone-deep chill at the Cuckoo's decline. The numbers of this iconic summer migrant have dropped by 65% since the early 1980s.

There are several breeding pairs at Wicken Fen and this is likely to be one of those individuals. Their targets are the nests of Reed Warbler, Meadow Pipit, Pied Wagtail and Dunnock. I saw one once as I walked on the fen, its wings sickle-shaped, the style of it somehow blending pigeon with House Martin and Sparrowhawk to create something other, its flight so different from Song Thrush, Jay or Rook that my brain couldn't categorise it. It was a shape of bird and a style of flying I had never seen.

The Cuckoo I can hear is calling half a mile or so distant and I cannot see it, but this is a significant moment for me. These birds are still here, still returning, their numbers are beleaguered but they cling on at Wicken. What does its future hold? Might the decreased use of neonicotinoids increase the populations of its insect prey, allowing more pairs to breed successfully? Might Brexit lead to a renewed use of these pernicious pesticides and threaten the Cuckoo still further? Either way I feel privileged to hear it, grateful that Wicken provides a haven for this struggling species and hopeful that this isn't the only one I'll hear this season.

WORDS – EMMA MITCHELL | **ART –** LISA PANNEK

Lesser Spotted Woodpecker

Dryobates minor

"I thought it would last my time," wrote Philip Larkin in his 1972 poem "Going, Going", a bruised, bitter elegy for a disappearing countryside. "But what do I feel now? Doubt?"

There is no room for uncertainty any more. Today they are winking out like stars, the cornfield annuals, the insects, the birds: some loudly fought for, some quietly mourned, some almost entirely unremarked. Outside birding circles, who will notice the loss of the tiny, shy Lesser Spotted Woodpecker? Who really cares if it goes?

Culturally, the 'lesser spot' isn't a bird we've paid proper attention to, and I wonder how that affects our chances of halting its decline. Like many ornithologists before and after him, C.A. Johns treated them purely as an addendum to their larger cousins: "It scarcely needs a lengthened description," he wrote in 1882's *British Birds in their Haunts*; "it is in all probability no less abundant, its smaller size rendering it less likely to be noticed." A smaller version of something else. No idea how many there are here. Next.

I think we had one once in our garden in Surrey, back when I was a child. There were Nuthatches in the willow and Treecreepers in the gnarled old apples; the badminton net was crusted with butterfly eggs, and in our attic three species of bat bred. My dad kept a heavy pair of binoculars on the kitchen windowsill along with a battered, spineless copy of the *Observer's Book of British Birds*, and I recall a lot of excitement about a woodpecker one weekend afternoon. I wish I could ask him about it so as to be sure it wasn't a Great Spotted Woodpecker that I remember, but dementia means that those long-ago days of natural abundance have long since faded from his mind.

And the bird itself is fading, along with so much else. The UK and European population of Lesser Spotted Woodpeckers has collapsed since 1980, when I was five. So few remain in Britain that annual monitoring is no longer possible: they could easily slip away without us ever quite knowing when. It's not persecution that's done it, or anything that can easily be reversed; we've simply altered the UK landscape to suit us, leaving hardly any room for these lovely, tiny birds.

"Most things are never meant," wrote Larkin, sadly; "This won't be, most likely… I just think it will happen, soon."

CHANGING BOCC STATUS 1–2–3–4

RED-LIST CRITERIA APPLICABLE
- IUCN Globally Threatened
- Historical breeding population decline
- Breeding population decline
- Non-breeding population decline
- Breeding range decline
- Non-breeding range decline

WORDS – MELISSA HARRISON | **ART –** RACHEL TOLL

Merlin

Falco columbarius

Birds of prey evoke a strong sense of place for me. When I think or talk about somewhere I've visited, I can't help but recall the raptors I encountered there. Similarly, if I'm thinking or talking about a specific species, I can't stop images playing in my head of the location and landscape of a memorable encounter I've experienced with that particular raptor.

The Merlin presents me with a set of such conflicting memories of vastly different geographic and social landscapes that are hard to reconcile, but it's one of the reasons why I think of this little falcon with such affection.

My first acquaintance with the Merlin takes me back to the remote Isle of Lewis in the Outer Hebrides in 2005. Employed as a field ecologist I spent months trudging in windswept solitude across vast sodden peatlands, mostly featureless aside from the occasional upturned vehicle carcass rusting into the peat. The cold ache of fieldwork was a constant reminder of my misery (the aftermath of a relationship break down was all consuming) but frequent encounters with nesting Merlins brought me back to earth and distracted from rain-heavy clothes and thoughts.

Frequently described as 'feisty' and 'dashing', their rapid fire "*kek, kek, kek, kek, kek, kek*" signalled a presence that demanded immediate attention. Binoculars raised, scanning for a flash of wing or tail, miniature Spitfires with acrobatic precision, even a glimpse was hard-won and savoured.

Fast forward six years and it's February and I'm in the USA. A colleague asked if I wanted to help him look for Merlins on the way in to work and obviously I said "yes". I imagined us taking a detour from the city and out into the wild-lands of Idaho then hiking out far from the beaten track to catch a fleeting glimpse of one of these pocket-sized predators, based on my experience on Lewis. What I did not expect was to spend the following hours cruising around the ghetto districts of Boise, listening to Lady GaGa (not my choice – but quite apt given this surreal fieldwork experience and my colleague said it helped us to blend into our surroundings) and finding migrant Merlins perching in small trees overlooking a neighbourhood of shacks, car-wrecks and discarded plastic toys.

The wide lonely landscape of Lewis couldn't be further from the inner city chaos of a Boise trailer park but the Merlin takes me back to both in an instant.

CHANGING BOCC STATUS 1–2–3–4

RED-LIST CRITERIA APPLICABLE

- IUCN Globally Threatened
- Historical breeding population decline
- Breeding population decline
- Non-breeding population decline
- Breeding range decline
- Non-breeding range decline

WORDS – RUTH TINGAY | **ART –** NATALIE TOMS

'Merlin Falcons'

Golden Oriole

Oriolus oriolus

CHANGING BOCC STATUS 1–2–3–4

RED-LIST CRITERIA APPLICABLE

- IUCN Globally Threatened
- Historical breeding population decline
- Breeding population decline
- Non-breeding population decline
- Breeding range decline
- Non-breeding range decline

Yodelling like a cowboy, the melody undulates from the tight, peach bill. Waves of tune that engulf and invigorate. Yet even a melody so bold and brilliant doesn't disclose the location of the Oriole. Leaves tremble. Wind or wing? A flash of yellow. Buttercup or bird? Tune diminishes. Silence.

The clear, cool air is sliced once again by a shard of melody that grows and unfurls unbidden. It rises and falls in waves; an aural rocking chair. Once again I peer through fern and thistle, craning and stretching, squinting and squinching. In that moment, I would do anything to see the slender Oriole slipping through the foliage. I would burst at the sight of the verdancy being broken by an explosion of buttercup-yellow and jet black.

Then, in a heart-shattering, breath-snatching moment I glimpse him. His melodious fluting seems to swell, balloon-like, and fill every crack and crevice until every ounce of me is ringing in tune, until every sense is trembling with anticipation. I am astounded by his grace. His blue-grey legs seem to propel him from twig to twig with an unparalleled athleticism. Then, the finale. Those slender yet deep maroon eyes seem almost to focus on me. They narrow and widen.

Bird and girl. We are two, yet we are alike. Our hearts both pound as we watch each other, our gazes both narrow and our breath quickens. Then he plucks a blade from the earth and returns home. He is a grass weaver, an artist, a soon-to-be-father. He is an avian angel and an unashamed soloist. He is bold and yet he is threatened.

Seeing a Golden Oriole? Perhaps it will never be. Perhaps not for me.

That imagined sighting is all I have to grasp onto. I fold it up tightly in my mind and hold onto it, like a warm penny in a fist. It is a thought so golden and sweet, like the glorious fluting of an Oriole. Yet it is remote and distant, like the plains of Africa where the Oriole resides during the chilled winter months. Maybe one day the land will once again echo with the elusive whistling of this glorious bird. Maybe one day I will have children and they will not have to watch, like I do, as the Golden Oriole slips down the ranks until it silently slips into oblivion, never to sing again.

WORDS – BELLA LACK | **ART –** WILL ROSE

WILL ROSE 2019

Red-backed Shrike

Lanius collurio

CHANGING BOCC STATUS 1–2–3–4

RED-LIST CRITERIA APPLICABLE

- IUCN Globally Threatened
- Historical breeding population decline
- Breeding population decline
- Non-breeding population decline
- Breeding range decline
- Non-breeding range decline

The Red-backed Shrike was not a shrike, it was an un-heeded canary. A bush perched bug butcher, a sentinel over heaths and plains; dumpy, chestnut-cloaked and smaller than a Song Thrush, the male's grey head and villainous black mask were fit for a masquerade.

Victorian shrikes watched over the land from Durham to Devon and Kent to Conway; eyes alert for burly bumblebees, dumpy dung beetles, well-fed wasps, even delicious lizards. With a pounce and swoop the animal was dead in the shrike's little raptorial bill. Then the autograph deed: animals impaled on thorns or barbs to make a hanging larder.

By the time the Beatles arrived our shrike was in rapid retreat, gone from extensive to elusive; only about 250 pairs, scattered in south-east England. Declines continued, by the Thatcher years the shrike was teetering on the edge of national extinction. In 1989 it was down to one heath, with one nest in one short lonely lolly-pop tree, and one watcher standing proud, binoculars at attention. In the morning the nest was empty, how did the eggers find the nest everybody wondered?

"Actually the little bird's extirpation was caused by the weather", experts opined, with vague authority. But seminal RSPB ornithologist Colin Bibby, writing in 1973, saw it clearly "the availability of food for the Red-backed Shrike … has presumably been the proximate cause of its decline. … Large moths have decreased by about two-thirds at Rothamstead since about 1948. Allusions to the loss of grasshoppers and butterflies … have been so frequent that they may well be true. … bumblebees and some beetles, could well have decreased unnoticed. Changes in numbers of many such species, if they have really occurred, may have climatic causes, but fragmentation of their habitat by the cultivation of waste ground, changes in grazing patterns, or the use of pesticides may have been important."

The Red-backed Shrike was our insectivore alarm call, but it's taken us half a century to respond to the collapse in insect bioabundance. Our shrike has not done with us yet; an occasional sprinkle arrives on spring migration, and, rarely, a pair will nest, indeed they even did so in northerly Shetland in 2015. Essentially fleeting visits, but the main excitement centres on a Dartmoor valley where, in insect friendly scrub and flower-rich rhos pasture, away from heavily grazed moorland, Red-backed Shrikes have often bred since 2007; in 2011 two pairs reared seven young. But the spark has yet to catch, we may first have to fix insect bioabundance before we have a shrike comeback.

WORDS – MATT SHARDLOW | **ART –** CARL SEEBODE

Willow Tit

Poecile montanus

The late Bill Condry said of what's often referred to by birdwatchers as "the confusion pair" that "It would be the greatest help … if these two remarkably similar birds, the Marsh and Willow Tits, occupied entirely separate parts of the country. Instead, their ranges are so mixed up you can expect to find either in many parts of Wales." Actually, the scientific names give a clue to the likeliest distinguishing habitats: Marsh Tit is *Poecile palustris*, whilst Willow Tit is *Poecile montanus*.

They are indeed quite difficult to distinguish from each other – an ultimate ornithological badge-test. Voice is a better guide here than appearance, the Willow Tit's being the less percussive, the more musical – though if you're lucky enough to be visited by a group of Willow Tits, you'll also be struck by their more dapper appearance, overall grey sheen of the plumage beautifully contrasted with the matt-black cap. The behavior too is distinctive. Catch a pair of small birds excavating a nest hole in a rotten willow, and our subject is the likeliest culprit (though to confuse matters, Marsh Tits may take it over in subsequent years).

My favourite places for seeing them, in little, hectic, tuneful groups of half-a-dozen or so, darting around and clinging to willow-poles, are the carrs on the way up to Bury Ditches in Shropshire's hill-country. North of there I've seen none; here, like much else, they may live on forever. Early birders – Yarrell in his *History of British Birds* (1843), and W.H. Hudson in his *British Birds* (1895) – in writing on Marsh Tits describe behaviour clearly that of Willow Tits. It would be unfair to blame Hudson or Yarrell for this, as the Willow Tit was not added to the British list until 1900, questions around its status only having been resolved in 1897. One of the more recent additions to that list, Red-listed now they seem fated to fade out of existence again.

My frequent sightings of this exquisite little bird and poignant songster (think Wood Warbler's elegiac tones) around Clun tally with Condry's observation that "upstream from Newbridge on Wye you are more likely to see Willow Tits than Marsh Tits; but nearer Builth where the riverside trees are greater and the soils richer, there you enter Marsh Tit country". Go further north, and they disappear again. So much about birdlife is still inexplicable, but I hope they hang on in this sublime stronghold.

CHANGING BOCC STATUS 1–2–3–4

RED-LIST CRITERIA APPLICABLE

- IUCN Globally Threatened
- Historical breeding population decline
- Breeding population decline
- Non-breeding population decline
- Breeding range decline
- Non-breeding range decline

WORDS – JIM PERRIN | **ART –** MAX ANGUS

38

Marsh Tit

Poecile palustris

The woodland here floods in winter, the volume of water too great for the river that marks the wood's eastern boundary. The wood itself never really dries out, the ground damp throughout the summer and the air heavy with moisture and the buzz of invertebrate life. Moving around the wood is difficult; unmanaged, the fallen limbs create a tangle that hinders movement and disorientates the casual visitor, though seemingly not the ever-present Muntjac. It is here that I come to find and monitor nests, mostly those of thrushes and Wrens, but also Marsh Tits, which seek out suitable cavities within the ageing timber.

Unlike Willow Tit, Marsh Tit does not excavate its own hole – though it may sometimes enlarge one to make it more suitable. This behavioural difference can prove a useful identification feature, the two species so closely matched in their appearance. Both species used to breed locally, though the collapse of Willow Tit populations across East Anglia means that I rarely encounter the species these days. While the Marsh Tits are still here, I struggle with the nagging sense that they are in decline. Such negative thoughts are borne out by the stark figures published in *Bird Atlas 2007–11*, which records a 22% reduction in breeding range since 1968/72, when the first national breeding atlas survey was carried out.

Our woodland is changing, becoming more fragmented in nature and altered by shifting management practices and increased grazing pressure from a growing population of introduced deer. Marsh Tits favour woodlands with a complex understorey and require surprisingly large patches of suitable habitat in order to breed successfully. Within this block of wet woodland they seem to be holding their own, a pair or two evident each year and revealed by their distinctive "*pitchoo*" alarm call, often replaced by "*tchee-tchee*" around the nest.

Marsh Tits can be wary around the nest, far more so than Blue Tit or Great Tit, with my local individuals sometimes reluctant to approach a nest site when a small camera is in position just a few metres away. That there is sufficient food for the chicks is suggested from the camera's images, showing the birds arriving with beaks full of small caterpillars. However, such casual evidence needs to be viewed with caution; Marsh Tit laying dates are now, on average, some 10 days earlier than they were in the 1960s, a likely effect of changing climate and something that might just alter the delicate balance in timing between the peak food demands of growing chicks and peak availability for suitable caterpillar prey.

CHANGING BOCC STATUS 1–2–3–4

RED-LIST CRITERIA APPLICABLE

- IUCN Globally Threatened
- Historical breeding population decline
- Breeding population decline
- Non-breeding population decline
- Breeding range decline
- Non-breeding range decline

WORDS – MIKE TOMS | **ART –** KATIE FULLER

1/8
Marsh tit

39

Skylark

Alauda arvensis

CHANGING BOCC STATUS 1–2–3–4

RED-LIST CRITERIA APPLICABLE
- IUCN Globally Threatened
- Historical breeding population decline
- Breeding population decline
- Non-breeding population decline
- Breeding range decline
- Non-breeding range decline

I spent more than 40 years living with a passionate birder. We met in the bird observatory on Fair Isle, so I understood a little of the obsession. Our first year of marriage was spent in Wales, while Tim was helping to warden birds of prey, then we moved to the Wirral, where we were the only residents of the tidal island of Hilbre. I should have known what I was taking on.

Even so, the depth of his passion came as a continual surprise, as I followed him on BTO surveys and got dragged round the country on twitches. I could enjoy the cute birds – the Puffins and the Storm-petrels – and the flashy ones like Goldfinches and Kingfishers, but was always slightly bemused that he could take such pleasure in the boring little brown birds, no matter how rare they were or how apparently interesting their behaviour. The sparrows, the pipits and larks left me cold.

While I couldn't understand Tim's delight in these species, however, I could share his pleasure in the places they were found. I saw more of the country than I ever would have done without him. In the 1980s his work with the RSPB took us to the North East. We moved to Northumberland and I fell in love with the wild, empty places, the magnificent coastline and especially the uplands. I learned to look out for the first Wheatear of the year and there was a real excitement in finding my own Ring Ouzel on a rocky outcrop. But the bird that came to represent for me those uplands, the hills of my adopted county, was the Skylark. It didn't matter that it looked rather boring, brown and streaky. Usually I only saw it, high in the sky, from below. Its amazing song, which has often been captured in story and music, lifted my spirits. It felt like a celebration of space and of light.

The flight of the male bird is spectacular. It rises almost vertically from the ground, then hovers effortlessly, sometimes for an hour or more, before plunging back to earth. It's a tragedy that this iconic bird is under threat. It's endangered because its habitat ranges beyond the moors and into cultivated farmland. The spread of intensive agriculture has limited the species' opportunities for breeding.

The Skylark is far from brown and boring. It's a joyous representation of my home.

WORDS – ANN CLEEVES | **ART –** RORY MCCANN

Wood Warbler

Phylloscopus sibilatrix

Tottenham is my motherland. I ain't into football it's just the place I grew up and where my love for this wing-shaking, trilling-singing, 'phyllosc' starts. The beautiful Wood Warbler. One of my first birding memories was going to get my hair cut with my dad walking through Bruce Castle Park when an Oystercatcher flew over calling. That was amazing, a seaside bird flying over the middle of Tottenham!

Back in the 1980s, Wood Warblers were disappearing in the London area quicker than a Brexit deal in 2019. The year before my father had been to Great Northaw Wood, Hertfordshire and managed to hear a singing Wood Warbler. I turned up the following week with him and nothing! The following spring my father returned early from his pre-work morning walk around Bruce Castle Park; he didn't gently open the door, he burst through shouting "Wood Warbler in the park!" There was moment of stillness and then I sprang into action; we legged it and charged down the park, possibly breaking all land speed records (in my mind at least).

There, at the south end of the park, next door to the museum, in the triangle of Silver Birch trees was a beautiful, wing-quivering, tail-shaking, lemon-dipped, bright olive-backed, I can't-sing-loud-enough, stonking Wood Warbler! The mythical warbler I'd hoped to see one day in some Beech tree-ridden wood somewhere in Wales or Scotland was just here, in Tottenham. We watched it flit amongst the branches singing nearly all the time. It was sensational! I'd never dreamed it would be this good. So yellow on the throat, so silvery white below and so, so, so green above! Let alone all those dark feather centres to the remiges. The song! The song was so much better than I'd expected. Starting like a ball bouncing until it gets closer and closer to the ground before bursting into a beautiful trill. Dropping the odd "*pew, pew*" call was just the best thing ever! So eventually I headed off to school and my dad off to work.

So this wasn't just a one off; every year or three one would turn up again. As I met more London birders, I'd put the news out and some were twitched to my delight. In autumn they often turned up and in 1989 I managed three different birds! Does it get any better than that? Only when I jammed into the odd Pied Flycatcher...

CHANGING BoCC STATUS 1–2–3–4

RED-LIST CRITERIA APPLICABLE

- IUCN Globally Threatened
- Historical breeding population decline
- Breeding population decline
- Non-breeding population decline
- Breeding range decline
- Non-breeding range decline

WORDS – DAVID DARRELL-LAMBERT | **ART –** EMILY TULL

EMT'19

Grasshopper Warbler

Locustella naevia

CHANGING BOCC STATUS 1–2–3–4

RED-LIST CRITERIA APPLICABLE

- IUCN Globally Threatened
- Historical breeding population decline
- Breeding population decline
- Non-breeding population decline
- Breeding range decline
- Non-breeding range decline

Not much bigger than a Blue Tit, this small, shy bird resembles the Sedge Warbler, with dark flecking and a broad tail. At first it might seem like its tuneful trilling is a lost cicada blown north by the wind.

The 'Brake Hopper', 'Reeler' or 'Cricket Bird', as it is variously known in the UK, is often only noticed when singing. Usually skulking in bushes and reeds, with its olive-brown striated plumage it seems to melt into its surroundings. In the late 18th century, naturalist parson Gilbert White described it as a "most artful creature, skulking in the thickest part of a bush; and will sing at a yard distance, and when undisturbed it sings at the top of a twig, gaping and shivering with its wings."

I'd only heard it before, and never seen it. Now here it was, clasped gently in the ringer's hand, giving itself up to be measured and recorded, and worth far more in the hand than it was in the reeds. A gentle blow on the breast lifted the feathers to reveal the bare muscle and flesh with just a little layer of yellow – the fatty tissue that would be vital to keep it going. Grasshopper Warblers leave their West African wintering grounds in early January and in spite of the challenges of vast Saharan journeys and windy sea crossings they arrive at reserves such as Titchfield Haven in Hampshire. Here, in one year, a remarkable 950 have been ringed. I saw mine at the far reaches of its range on the southern tip of Norway. Amongst the fertile coastline of shallow bays, wetland, moorland and heaths the exhausted warblers can find good feeding.

When the stream of song spills out from a bush or bramble clump at dawn or dusk it's often hard to find. The bird dissembles its location by rotating its head so that its song seems to shift, thrown about in many directions.

"Nothing can be more amusing than the whisper of this little bird which seems to be close by though at an hundred yards distance, and when close at your ear is scarce any louder than when a great way off." Gilbert White wrote.

This superb ventriloquist needs patience and careful stalking to track it down. When you finally set eyes on it, you can't help noticing its whole body vibrating with the effort of that reeling song.

WORDS – MIRIAM DARLINGTON | **ART –** DEREK ROBERTSON

Savi's Warbler

Locustella luscinioides

There are moments in the greatest sacred music when the majesty of the choir is silenced and in the calm that follows a single voice emerges, eloquent and impossibly pure, making sense of all that has gone before and taking the beauty of the music to a level that is almost unbearably sweet.

I had such a moment in the Maytime dawn in 2017. It's always easy to find an excuse for not getting up at 3.30, but at last I managed it, creeping out of the house fully dressed for winter and clutching a flask of tea, to make the short journey to the marshes that lie just beyond my house on the edge of the Broads.

It was as it always was, as it always is. One by one the chorus swells until it's a mighty noise… the voices of birds coming from the darkness, getting louder and more numerous and now coming from dark greyness, reaching a climax in the pale greyness before the choir gently drops away, leaving pauses for the solo singers to make their statement.

At first I thought it was a Sedge Warbler, but the singer refused to spiral off into the infinite variety that this species loves. It continued with a gentle insistent whirring, as if from some humdrum mechanical source, and it was then that I knew where I was and I allowed myself a small, careful smile, one that did not for a second disturb the singing bird.

The sound is not, I suppose, particularly beautiful in itself. You need a little knowledge and background to get the most from it: to feel that sense of humility and privilege that comes from association with some rare thing. And more than that, you need to be sitting in the reeds before sun-up, colour slowly returning to the land and your head full of the wild beauty of song.

I never heard that bird again: a fleeting visit. It was a Savi's Warbler, a bird more often found in southern Europe and temperate west Asia; BTO notes that it gets around 10 records of this species in a year in Britain. That same week a Savi's also turned up at Minsmere and another at Titchwell… like some great singer with the perfect tour schedule: Carnegie Hall, Royal Albert Hall and my back garden.

CHANGING BOCC STATUS 1–2–3–4

RED-LIST CRITERIA APPLICABLE

- IUCN Globally Threatened
- Historical breeding population decline
- Breeding population decline
- Non-breeding population decline
- Breeding range decline
- Non-breeding range decline

WORDS – SIMON BARNES | **ART –** IAN MICHAEL CLAXTON

Aquatic Warbler

Acrocephalus paludicola

Aquatics you may guess are fond of mire and fen
Yet sodden earth's not enough for chicks to fledge
Now they pass endless fields made by men
And migrate 'til reaching vast tracts of sedge.

But what's an Aquatic you may well ask!
For they're rare enough to elicit birder's hype
Sometimes accompanied by a chorus of gasps
Is it a Sedgie? No! I saw a central head stripe!

Storms may roll in but Aquatic's aren't fazed
Above the thunder rivals chatter and serenade
Neighbouring Elk pass hidden nests to graze
Below grassy thickets eggs stealthily are laid.

But oh! the misfortune of being a specialist today!
To rely on subsidies and management to persist
Please can we keep traditional ways of making hay?
Yet, the Anthropocene favours the generalist.

Their whistles and chatter mayn't be heard for long
Between drumming of Snipe and Elk's hefty stomp
Future generations deprived of nature's song
Unless we protect precious marsh, mire and swamp.

CHANGING BOCC STATUS 1–2–3–4

RED-LIST CRITERIA APPLICABLE

- IUCN Globally Threatened
- Historical breeding population decline
- Breeding population decline
- Non-breeding population decline
- Breeding range decline
- Non-breeding range decline

WORDS – ALICE RISELY | **ART –** COLIN BLANCHARD

1/20 'Habitat'

Marsh Warbler

Acrocephalus palustris

An odd choice of bird to write about maybe, as I have never actually seen one – only heard one… once! Frustrating as that may sound, it doesn't matter – and just goes to show how fascinating a bird can be, despite being so rare and elusive. I have come to regard this little bird as a challenge… and that one day I might get to see one.

I came to birding quite late in life and so I often rely on more knowledgeable colleagues to help me catch up on bird ID, so it was only with the help of an experienced birder that I even got to hear my first (and only) Marsh Warbler. As with so many small brown birds, it's the song that is most remarkable. It's not their own song – rather a 'top 100' compilation of the various British species that it's heard over the summer, mixed with another 100 or so African species it has heard whilst abroad; all downloaded, combined, and intertwined to produce a most wonderful sound – it's like the dawn chorus condensed into a single bird.

When they're not singing, identification can be a real problem and I can honestly say that if I did ever get to see one, I'd really struggle to distinguish it from a Reed Warbler as they look so similar (my challenge gets more and more difficult!). The saving grace is that the habitat should help as Marsh Warblers tend to ignore reed and prefer thick vegetation.

So why write about a bird that I have never seen? Well, that just goes to show what a struggle these birds face. They have never really done that well in the UK and now they are virtually extinct with barely a handful of breeding pairs in south-eastern England. We don't fully understand why their numbers have plummeted so low in recent years and therefore it's hard to know what to do to help them. Such are the challenges with conservation.

Still, they're very much on 'my list' of birds I'd like to see one day… I might be walking in Kent and hear that beautiful song again… I will have my binoculars at the ready!

CHANGING BOCC STATUS 1–2–3–4

RED-LIST CRITERIA APPLICABLE
- IUCN Globally Threatened
- Historical breeding population decline
- Breeding population decline
- Non-breeding population decline
- Breeding range decline
- Non-breeding range decline

WORDS – MIRANDA KRESTOVNIKOFF | **ART –** CHRIS ORGILL

Translucent with light
In an area of dense vegetation
which was drenched after a
heavy shower. The song amazing
Sedge and Reed Warbler, a little
Goldfinch and an assortment of calls.
Hidden but audible for long periods
showed well at times over a long
period of watching.
CHRIS ORGILL

45

Starling

Sturnus vulgaris

We forget that you were once as common as coal; little coal-black bird.
Stumpy, dumpy. The wire-dotter; pylon-swarmer.
Camped out on our ledges and trees, screaming England's towns down.
Noisy as a classroom on the last day of term.
We forget that you once shimmered through frozen air; ripple bird.
Shape-shifter, dusk-dancer. Murmurer; sky-writer,
Endlessly becoming in the darkening gold: animals, patterns, waves.
And how we, wonder-struck, witnessed your nightly unity against death.
We forget that you stayed true; loyal little bird.
Roof-flocker; aerial-clinger, when the rest up and left.
And how, up close, you carried the constellations in your feathers,
Iridescent purples, greens and blues, the rare hues of petrol on water.
We forget that you were once as common as coal; little coal-black bird.
And that your blackening of our streets and whistling through our chimneystacks,
Your smoke-like swirling in the skies, was an olive branch from heaven.
Yet in the mad pursuit of a spotless life, we believed you plague.
We forget that in loss it's the little things that leave the largest holes;
And that, all along, you were drawing patterns for us to live by:
Community bird, collaborator, congregator, conversation bird.
You, accepter bird, come-together bird.
Crowd bird. YOLO bird.
The dance-like-no-one's-watching bird,
Over town and field, city and sea.
Beauty-beyond-compare bird. Modest bird,
Youth bird. Joy bird.
We forget that you were once as common as coal,
And how that makes your scarcity more keenly felt.
And how losing you is devastating,
A hole in our sky and soul.
For it signifies a greater loss in us.

CHANGING BOCC STATUS 1–2–3–4

RED-LIST CRITERIA APPLICABLE
- IUCN Globally Threatened
- Historical breeding population decline
- Breeding population decline
- Non-breeding population decline
- Breeding range decline
- Non-breeding range decline

WORDS – ROB COWEN | **ART –** LIZA ADAMCZEWSKI

Ring Ouzel

Turdus torquatus

CHANGING BOCC STATUS 1–2–3–4

RED-LIST CRITERIA APPLICABLE
- IUCN Globally Threatened
- Historical breeding population decline
- Breeding population decline
- Non-breeding population decline
- Breeding range decline
- Non-breeding range decline

It's the thinking person's Blackbird, the connoisseur's choice; a passerine, that keeps itself to itself and is somewhat exclusive, hiding away from the cheap(ing) twittering masses of other perching birds, other than the odd corvid, Wheatear and pipit.

It sits aloof, inhabiting the rugged, broken landscapes of the upland. Here it can be highly secretive, but catch a moment and you might hear one of the most distinctive songs, the music of the wilds. A trisyllabic piping carries far on the wind. Get close and between these strident penetrating notes a more subtle melody can sometimes be heard whispered under its breath, a gentle warbling ... a Mistle Thrush in a small box.

The fact you have to invest some kind of effort to find one makes them all the more appealing to me. Our only summer migrant thrush, it does occasionally make a celebrity appearance far from the sheepwalk, heath and the clitter. When on migration they can pop up almost anywhere, from the beach, urban park or golf course. It was such a moment when this bird dropped into my life for the first time. Camping on the Isle of Wight in September, I recall vividly my dad coming into the tent after an early morning walk, excitedly exclaiming he thought he'd just seen a Ring Ouzel. I had never heard of such a beast; it certainly sounded weird. A scramble in the glove compartment of my dad's Mark 1 Vauxhall Cavalier for a copy of the *Shell Book of British Birds* (you know the one ...) and his identification was confirmed.

A bird, sitting proud with a Persil-white gorget – this was a bird even I could identify, so I headed off to where the sighting had occurred: an elderberry bush, growing from a wall on a grassy path en route to the beach. I sprinted down, just in time to convince myself I saw it flick itself over the wall and out of sight. If I'm honest I was self-stringing, if this is even a term? I can't be sure now that what I saw wasn't just another Blackbird, the Ouzel's common and closest relative.

Another subtlety about this bird is that unless you get a good look at it from the front no-one but a hardened birder would recognise the longer-look or the silvered underwing; it looks to the untrained eye just like a Blackbird. This first moment, real or imagined, was enough to set me off; my love for this bird is partly what led me to live where I do now on Dartmoor, where a population just about hangs on. A situation that is about as delicate as the frosted feather edges on the bird's breast. But for now at least, I know there are places where the spirit of the uplands rides on the wind and pushes through the murk and the mizzle.

WORDS – NICK BAKER | **ART –** PAUL THOMAS

© Paul Thomas -
-2019- after
AUBREY BEARDSLEY-
HOW. A. CONFIDING. RING. OUZEL. LIFTED.
YE. BLUE. KNIGHT'S. SPIRITS. AND. SHIT.

Fieldfare

Turdus pilaris

The Fieldfare edges onto the British Red List on the most tentative of pretexts. Its British breeding population has declined in recent years from a handful of pairs to but one or two. Yet these two toehold pairs of Fieldfares, and their status, do not reflect the meaning of this bird in British lives.

In his tender, wonderful *Bird Therapy* my friend Joe Harkness recounts his elation when two Fieldfares (Britain's entire breeding population, I like to imagine) visit his garden, driven by ice and snow. Joe's joy comes not from the beauty of the birds, though beautiful they certainly are, nor from their rarity, for per se they are not rare at all (globally they are listed by BirdLife International as being of 'Least Concern'). His joy comes from their shining wildness, perceived – this once – in a place of domesticity. For Fieldfares are not birds of small gardens. Nor, despite their name, are they birds of dull, tamed British fields.

Rather, Fieldfares are birds of the lead and iron late October sky, which bears them from the north. As they come – these fierce-faced Valkyries – they drop their welly-squelch calls to earth. Next they themselves materialise from the cloud, stroking the wind with their too-large wings, stalling and guiding their fall with their black square tails. Like that the Nordic summer, the Green Sandpiper's song, the shrill whine of midges and the Crane's yell fall to the sad mud and the autumn-tousled grass of Britain. In the being of a bird.

They stay with us, the winter long, a million of these messengers of Wotan. They skip and chatter through the fog-wet hawthorn hedgetops as you walk. They strip Sea-Buckthorn bushes in the dunes, cold yellow bills and warm-flushed speckled chests glowing in the orange berries' fiery light.

This spring, in April, Fieldfares moved in waves above my morning dog walks, their voices urgent for the taiga. In the wake of their wings they dragged the winter sky, the cloud, the cold, leaving a warm space to be peopled instead by African voices. The taiga called the Fieldfares home, to sing with Serafina Pekkala, and each to claim a towering spruce from which to shout in anger at the soft-pawed coming of the marten and the Wolf.

CHANGING BOCC STATUS 1-2-3-4

RED-LIST CRITERIA APPLICABLE
- IUCN Globally Threatened
- Historical breeding population decline
- Breeding population decline
- Non-breeding population decline
- Breeding range decline
- Non-breeding range decline

WORDS – NICK ACHESON | **ART –** JO BROWN

Song Thrush

Turdus philomelos

CHANGING BOCC STATUS 1–2–3–4

RED-LIST CRITERIA APPLICABLE

- IUCN Globally Threatened
- Historical breeding population decline
- Breeding population decline
- Non-breeding population decline
- Breeding range decline
- Non-breeding range decline

Scillonian cream teas often come with a Song Thrush. Bold as brass, they come perch atop your table, sit next to you on the bench or bustle around your feet, hungrily eyeing up crumbs on plates. Around the small Isles of Scilly archipelago, from field edges to gardens, from tea rooms to maritime heathlands, Song Thrushes are plentiful and visible. First time Scilly holidaymakers often comment on their vitality. You hear it mentioned in passing on tripper boats and in pubs. The birds seem indivisible from the landscape. It all seems a touch confusing, disarming, unexpected. Stepping back in time to a more innocent age.

Plain brown on top, cream underneath with dark spots across the breast and a black inquisitive eye, this thrush may not be a natural beauty, but wait until he opens his lungs. Throughout the spring, you'll hear the Song Thrushes start up across the islands, serenading in the morning with a captivating tune, usually made up of musical phrases repeated in threes. They're marking their territory, wooing a mate, fending off rivals – to us it's simply singing.

Song Thrushes are thriving on Scilly. Farming here is still largely managed in the traditional manner. Small fields, varied crops, tall hedges as windbreaks and no pesticides create the perfect nesting and foraging environment for some garden birds in peril elsewhere. They're boosted by a mild climate and no native mammalian predators. Invertebrates and berries abound, giving the birds much needed vitamins amongst their artificial diet of scones and cakes. They must dread the low season when some of the cafes close. No longer tame throstles on welfare performing for tourists, they must dig deep to recall what it means to be a wild bird: "Crack, it had caught a snail and was knocking it on the stone. Crack! Crack!", enthused J.R.R. Tolkien in *The Hobbit*.

Scilly has one of the densest populations of Song Thrushes anywhere in the UK – perhaps 1,000+ pairs. They are thriving on island life. However, since the 1960s we have lost a million pairs of Song Thrush nationally in an age of chemical farming, uprooted hedgerows, tidied edgelands, manicured lawns and snail pellet confetti. They are largely gone from the landscapes of home. Head to the Isles of Scilly on holiday then, to experience their confident abundance and reflect awhile on their loss from your daily life back on the mainland.

But, the Song Thrushes of Scilly care not a jot if you put the jam or the cream on the scone first, just that you do so in a cavalier sloppy way.

WORDS – LUCY MCROBERT AND ROB LAMBERT | **ART –** RICHARD ALLEN

49 Redwing

Turdus iliacus

Birds, for me, were a discovery of necessity. Something to look for on family rambles, something to 'collect' when my football sticker album was full, something to draw on rainy days in the caravan. Raptors were my obsession; all crazy-eyes and pointy bits, effortlessly cool yet lethal. And the improbably plumed; the kingfishers and rollers, orioles and bee-eaters. For hours I would pore over books whilst neglecting the text, convinced I would stumble upon a Wallcreeper in the school yard or a Lammergeier smashing tortoises in the local park.

Later, as a young adult, I learned more about birds and their habits and discovered that many are remarkable and they aren't always the snazziest. Birds that fly 18,000 mile round-trips only landing to nest. Songbirds that can walk underwater. The nomadic birds that arrive to lift our spirits when the days become cold and short. Birds like the Redwing.

The attractive-but-not-spectacular Redwing is the UK's smallest thrush, a tiny population of which breeds in the Scottish Highlands but over a million flock to our shores from Scandinavia and continental Europe each autumn. Moving overhead at night their ethereal voices proclaim their presence in the darkness even when they cannot be seen. They herald the onset of winter and many of us look forward to this event as much as some anticipate their first Swift of summer.

Targeting hedgerows and fields they forage for berries and worms, but colder snaps can drive them towards our gardens. During one such spell a few years ago I trudged down my street, wellies ploughing the thick, crunchy snow to find two Redwings battling fiercely on the ground. Desperately flailing and pecking, engrossed in their fight, they completely ignored me as I approached. Slowly reaching down I gently separated them, and for several wonderful moments I stood with an exhausted, scraggy warrior-Redwing in the palm of each hand. I watched their breath in the crisp air until they came to their senses and went their separate ways.

Each year, when our paths cross and I hear those first thin "*seep seep*" flight-calls of Redwings in the starlit sky, I close my eyes to listen and briefly, on some ancient level, we connect. For me, connections to the natural world like this are precious; they are moments to cherish, to share and hand down, not glean from books. And they are vital if we hope to make a difference to our dwindling bird populations.

CHANGING BOCC STATUS 1-2-3-4

RED-LIST CRITERIA APPLICABLE
- IUCN Globally Threatened
- Historical breeding population decline
- Breeding population decline
- Non-breeding population decline
- Breeding range decline
- Non-breeding range decline

WORDS – KIT JEWITT | **ART –** IAN RENDALL

Ian Rendall 2019

Mistle Thrush

Turdus viscivorus

CHANGING BOCC STATUS

RED-LIST CRITERIA APPLICABLE
- IUCN Globally Threatened
- Historical breeding population decline
- Breeding population decline
- Non-breeding population decline
- Breeding range decline
- Non-breeding range decline

Here's to the overlooked elder brother. The geeky, gawky, beer-bellied beanpole who's less good in company. The shy child excused games, hopping by itself in the middle of an empty playing field. Mistle Thrushes suffer in every way from comparison with their Song Thrush siblings. But I know which one I prefer.

As a fledgling birder in 2005, I found myself on High Peak in Derbyshire, trying to identify a grey-brown flock. They shuttled, undulating, from ground to tree and back again, flashing their underarms, white like the residue from roll-on deodorant. My field guide reading, streets ahead of my experience in the actual field, told me it was a classic mark. Twenty-seven of them, still the largest flock I've ever met. I saw my first Stonechat 20 minutes later.

Big, (the Swedish name is 'Dubbeltrast', the 'Double Thrush'), upright, defiant, with a back of a colour that Farrow & Ball would call Mouse Waistcoat and charge you a lot for. 'Mistle', because Mistletoe supposedly "sprang from the seed voided by the thrush". The scientific name means 'devourer of Mistletoe' – here they mostly go for Holly or hawthorn; often their defence of a Holly bush is the reason we still have berries at Christmas. They breed early and sing early; the old name 'Jeremy Joy' is a corruption of 'January joy'. A Mistle Thrush will defend territory whatever the weather, hence their dialect name 'storm-cock'. Also 'screech-cock', which is unfair. And in Scotland 'Big Mavis', which I'm going to use from now on.

The Mistle is Britain's largest warbling bird, and uses its resonant chest well. The song is loud, carrying, hurried then hesitant, exploring subclauses like an absent-minded lecturer; a sibilant, minor, melancholy Blackbird. At Lynford Arboretum, Norfolk, in April, we sat under one at dawn for many minutes. The song ran ahead of us jagging and swerving, a German Expressionist version of brother Song's more user-friendly carols.

Their call is unmistakeable, an old-style football rattle, but that's where the football connection ends. The College of Arms blazoned the badge granted to West Bromwich Albion in 1975 as "a Mistle Thrush perched on a raspberry branch". The herald was doubly misinformed. The branch is hawthorn, named after West Brom's ground, and the bird is a Song Thrush.

We found two carrying nest twigs in Islington on our BTO Breeding Atlas survey, and were very pleased. Even then I knew they were in decline.

WORDS – SAMUEL WEST | **ART –** CARRY AKROYD

Spotted Flycatcher

Muscicapa striata

The Spotted Flycatcher is, I reckon, a good candidate for a name change. *Muscicapa* – the generic name – is fine. It can stay. But I think '*familiaris*' gets much closer to describing the Spotted Flycatcher's character than does *striata*.

Of all the UK's Red-listed birds, few are as closely associated with gardens, churchyards and parks as '*Muscicapa familiaris*'. And unlike the noisy House Sparrows piling into your privet hedge, or the noisier Starlings bickering over your bread crusts, '*Muscicapa familiaris*' brings grace and refinement. If you're lucky, she's quietly nesting in your Ivy-clad wall, having confused your garden for a sylvan glade. Not to say that she's easy to see, but compared to Corncrakes, Slavonian Grebes, and her Pied cousins, well …

Despite this familiarity, I can't remember my first encounter with a Spotted Flycatcher, nor (more worryingly) my last. Whenever I do see one there's a feeling of surprise at remembering they even exist. Wikipedia describes her as "undistinguished" and "dull". "Lacking obvious features", according to Lars Svensson. "A bit boring" claim the RSPB (who, to their credit, go on to qualify: "beautiful in an understated way").

Easily overlooked, and (to my shame!) easily forgotten.

Scrolling through photographs of the Spotted Flycatcher, I'm struggling to match them up to any specific memory. But these still images fail entirely to capture the true essence of the thing. As soon as I picture their sallying, fly-catching leaps from an exposed branch into the humming woodland air, the memories start flitting back. In my mind's eye, it's still hard to picture the bird itself; but the places and the experiences are more vivid. English gardens, Scottish woods, French farms.

The Spotted Flycatcher remains pretty widespread across the UK, but this ubiquity masks a shocking decline in abundance, which fell by 87% between 1967 and 2016. According to BTO, the most likely driver of this decline is a reduction in the survival of first year birds. What's less clear is whether this is caused by processes operating during the British summer, on passage through Europe and North Africa, or over 'winter' in the humid African forests. It's likely that this inter-continental lifestyle makes the Spotted Flycatcher more vulnerable to human-caused environmental change; it certainly makes the task of diagnosing problems more challenging.

Here's hoping that conservationists at home and abroad can turn things around for '*Muscicapa familiaris*' before my memory fades altogether.

CHANGING BOCC STATUS 1–2–3–4

RED-LIST CRITERIA APPLICABLE

- IUCN Globally Threatened
- Historical breeding population decline
- Breeding population decline
- Non-breeding population decline
- Breeding range decline
- Non-breeding range decline

WORDS – TOM FINCH | **ART –** JONATHAN POMROY

Nightingale

Luscinia megarhynchos

CHANGING BOCC STATUS 1–2–3–4

RED-LIST CRITERIA APPLICABLE
- IUCN Globally Threatened
- Historical breeding population decline
- Breeding population decline
- Non-breeding population decline
- Breeding range decline
- Non-breeding range decline

Writing this sees me join a long list of people who have attempted to put the Nightingale into words over the last few thousand years.

Pliny the Elder, two thousand or so years ago described the song perfectly, an anonymous writer in the 12th century immortalised the "sooty brown ball" of a Nightingale in *The Owl and the Nightingale*, Shakespeare's Juliet educated Romeo of the night-time songster, Keats and Coleridge romanticised over its famous song, Mabey writes of his encounters with Nightingales singing from the shell craters of Salisbury Plain to the Dordogne valley. And now here's me.

I can't really describe how a Nightingale makes me feel. I'm not going to attempt to put its song into words. Last night I drove through Sussex, through my closed windows I heard the unmistakeable pipes and whistles. Over the past few weeks my life has been ruled by my quest to document the Nightingale's tale yet its siren-like song again drew me in.

In a daze I stepped from my car and was drawn to the scrub. In the distance another's song drifted through the darkness; my Nightingale sang, it sang and sang, up to the skies. I stood and listened, mesmerised by a song that has remained unchanged for millennia, I was hearing what Pliny would have heard. Whether it was as successful as attracting a mate as it was as attracting me from the road we will never know.

For centuries the Nightingale's was seen as a sorrowful song, yet to me it shouts of defiance and joy. However defiant its song may be though, its situation is now full of sorrow. To think that this bird, this bird that was (and still is by some) adored, versified and in some ways worshipped – after all countless pilgrims have travelled to be enraptured by its notes – is now on the brink, we should be ashamed that in our quest to clean our landscape, in our acrimonious divorce from nature, we have forgotten this songster and let it suffer. Despite its song we have ignored it; we have let it fall silent in our copses, our scrub and our hedgerows. We have failed it and with that we have failed nature. Will we really let this be the last song of the Nightingale?

WORDS – LUKE MASSEY | **ART –** JOHN FOKER

53 Pied Flycatcher

Ficedula hypoleuca

CHANGING BOCC STATUS 1–2–3–4

RED-LIST CRITERIA APPLICABLE

- IUCN Globally Threatened
- Historical breeding population decline
- Breeding population decline
- Non-breeding population decline
- Breeding range decline
- Non-breeding range decline

My story with Pied Flycatchers started when I was 20. Unemployed and on a government back to work scheme at Yarner Wood, Devon, I was set to monitor nest boxes. Firstly I encountered the nests. Neat and tidy bowls of brown dry oak leaves and grasses. Next the clutches of pale blue eggs. Then intimate encounters with the adults; making eye contact with a sitting female as she patiently waited for me to lower the nest box lid. The male chipping loudly from a branch level with me. This alarm call would later become familiar as I learned, head down, to ring the nestlings.

Once the young fledged the adults vanished, reappearing again the following April. Many of these birds later returned to Yarner Wood, but where they went between breeding seasons was a mystery.

Fifteen years later I returned a qualified scientist, trained in the Netherlands to fit new tiny tracking devices. Back in Devon we tagged some males. The year waiting for the tagged birds to return was an equal measure of excitement and worry, prolonged by the latest and coldest spring for 23 years. But then, yes!!! First one then another, they had made it. Over the following years we discovered that they migrate to a region of western Africa; Sierra Leone, Liberia, Guinea.

Four years on I am in Liberia with my student Fraser, and Emmanuel from the Liberian BirdLife partner SCNL. Mission – to start a Pied Flycatcher study to better understand the causes of their decline. With known locations of only four UK-ringed Pied Flycatchers ever found in the region, and with rough coordinates from the tracking work, our preselected site had drawn a blank – no Pied Flycatchers. Emmanuel suggested a wooded savannah in the north, rare habitat in an almost entirely forested country.

For days and days we drove and surveyed each morning, great birds but no Pied Flycatchers. We arrived at a village in the wooded savannah and after some discussion the villagers allowed us to stay. Early the next morning we walked the woodland edge playing the call. Bingo! At the first survey point, unmistakably, that alarm call – just like at Yarner. The male emerged from the forest edge to investigate. Success! That morning we found six more; we had found them! That was the easy part, our challenge now is to identify factors that are causing their decline.

WORDS – MALCOLM BURGESS | **ART –** DARREN WOODHEAD

Black Redstart

Phoenicurus ochruros

CHANGING BOCC STATUS 1–2–3–4

RED-LIST CRITERIA APPLICABLE

- IUCN Globally Threatened
- Historical breeding population decline
- Breeding population decline
- Non-breeding population decline
- Breeding range decline
- Non-breeding range decline

The Black Redstart, along with the House Sparrow and Feral Pigeon is seen as an emblematic urban bird in the UK. It is a bit of a dichotomy though, because although being almost exclusively tied to urban areas, in the grand scheme of things they are relatively unknown. Ask the average city dweller about them and I am certain you will receive more than your fair share of blank faces.

This species has always held a special allure for me. I first heard of Black Redstarts as a seven-year old whilst poring through the meagre half-shelf selection of books dedicated to natural history in my local library. On this occasion, I was thumbing through the pages of the minuscule *Observer's Book of Birds* when I stumbled across the page containing the monochrome illustration of a male and female Black Redstart. I noted with some excitement that it was a species that could be found in London. Perhaps I would see one at my then local patch – my back garden in Wembley, north London. I scurried home to start the vigil from my bedroom window.

My patient vigilance eventually paid off – well, sort off. On a spring morning some 13 years later I noticed a Common Redstart, the other redstart species to be found in the UK, hopping down my garden path. It was a lifer but not the fabled Black Redstart. However, I didn't have to wait much longer to see my fantasy bird because that winter I discovered a male along the fence line on the freezing windswept causeway at Staines Reservoir. It was worth the wait. I studied the bird closely and with much relish, almost as if I would never see another again.

Of course, I saw many thereafter at locations ranging from building sites in Wapping, east London, my current local patch at Wormwood Scrubs, to shopping centres in Manchester and upon perimeter walls at Dungeness, Kent. But I always wondered why they were among Britain's rarest birds – sometimes barely more than 40 breeding pairs in the whole country – whilst on continental Europe you are practically tripping over them in urban areas. One interesting supposition is that their numbers are kept low by competition with the far more dominant Robin. Whereas, on the Continent, the Robin is still largely a shy denizen of its natal woodlands and thus, due to the lack of competition in urban areas, Black Redstarts can thrive.

So next time you see a Black Redstart take a moment to savour this great bird. It is truly a unique urban gem.

WORDS – DAVID LINDO | **ART –** TIFFANY FRANCIS-BAKER

TIF

Whinchat

Saxicola rubetra

CHANGING BOCC STATUS 1–2–3–4

RED-LIST CRITERIA APPLICABLE

- IUCN Globally Threatened
- Historical breeding population decline
- Breeding population decline
- Non-breeding population decline
- Breeding range decline
- Non-breeding range decline

On 10th June 2013, a brood of six Whinchat chicks was colour-ringed as part of a Retrapping Adults for Survival (RAS) project on the RSPB reserve of Geltsdale in north Cumbria.

One of the brood had the ring combination of 'Lime' over 'Yellow' on the left leg and 'Green' over the metal BTO ring on the right leg. He became known as 'Lime/Yellow/Green/Metal' or 'LYGM'. Post-fledging, he moved several kilometres to a different part of the reserve and it was to here that he returned in 2014. From information gained from geo-tagged Whinchats in the Geltsdale population, it is likely he migrated down the west coast of Africa and spent the winter in one or more of the countries in sub-Saharan Africa before returning straight across the Sahara the following spring.

In 2014 he was eventually paired with a young colour-ringed female but no nest was found, so it is not known if they bred successfully. In 2015 he fledged three juveniles with a second female, but in 2016 he was with the 2014 female again and this time six juveniles fledged. His first partner in 2017 was his third female but they failed to nest successfully; later that season he fledged a brood with a fourth female. In 2018, five juveniles were fledged with his fifth female.

In June 2019 he became six years old and, therefore, one of the oldest known Whinchats. As with every year from 2014 onwards he set up his territory in the same area, fledging six young with a sixth female. Just before this brood fledged he was discovered with a seventh female at another nest about 500 m away. About two weeks after his first brood the second brood fledged, this time of four young. Meanwhile, female six moved and had another brood with a new male!

In six years LYGM has successfully fledged up to 30 juveniles – possibly more, several of which have returned as adults to breed – has been a bigamous male, has had late broods after initial failure and has travelled around 45,000 miles over 12 migrations. Sadly, despite his considerable contribution it is likely that the Whinchat population on the reserve has declined in the same six years of his existence.

WORDS – MARTIN KETCHER | **ART –** EMMA MURRAY

House Sparrow

Passer domesticus

CHANGING BOCC STATUS 1-2-3-4

RED-LIST CRITERIA APPLICABLE

- IUCN Globally Threatened
- Historical breeding population decline
- Breeding population decline
- Non-breeding population decline
- Breeding range decline
- Non-breeding range decline

From a garden on the edge of the green belt, nature was steadily removed. No longer any thistles and thorns, or the song of Skylark and display of Lapwing, only tarmac, brick, and human noise, but some species adapted and thrived.

The House Sparrow was my first close encounter with birds at home, feeding on a giant fatball feeder my dad had hung for me, retreating into my grandma's weeping willow at any sign of movement or danger. Very few species visited the garden, with the House Sparrows only accompanied by those other urban explorers, Starling, Woodpigeon, Blue Tit, and Sparrowhawk.

The House Sparrow flock was constantly present, making themselves known by their communal racket, a hidden gig amongst the twisted and curled branches of the willow, on an invite-only entry. What sounded like hundreds of birds, chatting, fighting, flitting from branch to branch, and only showing themselves when they had a breather on the uppermost branches. On approach a deadly silence would fall over the ruckus, or if they thought they had been rumbled, an explosion of wings, to the next venue.

The hierarchical, communal structure of the House Sparrow flock fascinated me; it reminded me of my time at school, the noise of the crowd, the hustle and bustle of breaks, and walks between lessons, chatting, football, friends, bullies and fights. Perfectly suited to the urban life, it felt as though the House Sparrows wore it proudly on their shoulders. The male's plumage complemented the planning authority's choice of colour scheme for our estate perfectly; the grey-blues of the crown – roof tiles and lead, the rufous tones of the nape – facia boards and brickwork, the browny-orange of the coverts – fences and window frames, and the black of the throat and eyes – tarmac and car tyres.

It always struck me as a strange concept that we build our houses communally, close together, in large estates, with only enough room to drag a wheelie bin between us, often not knowing our neighbours. It came as a pleasant surprise to find that our House Sparrows also adopted this lifestyle, nesting in the gaps and cracks of our houses, but showing a greater sense of community. They've even taken to terraced nest boxes, as we build nature un-friendly new homes, and fill our walls with cavity insulation. If we just give them a little space, House Sparrows can give everyone that feeling of the wild.

WORDS – CAIN SCRIMGEOUR | **ART –** STEPH THORPE

Tree Sparrow

Passer montanus

Nothing lifts my heart as much as watching a horde of Tree Sparrows swarming along a hedgerow, but sadly across much of the UK this is a thing of the past. The 93% decline between 1970 and 2008 has led to their absence from many areas, particularly in the south. There are many causes of this decline including changes in farming practice, loss of hedgerows and habitat loss through building developments.

They can be saved, especially if conservationists work with farmers. Tree Sparrows nest in hedgerows but they prefer holes and they readily take to nest boxes. In the summer the adults feed on seed and small invertebrates, including spiders, beetles, caterpillars and craneflies. The adults feed their young primarily on the invertebrates. In winter they feed on small seeds and we have found millet to be particularly attractive, so feeding this in feeders and planting conservation cover crops helps greatly.

Saving Tree Sparrows in Wiltshire has become a 20-year obsession that shows no sign of ending. Our research shows that some are sedentary, never moving from their natal site but others disperse in the first few months of life. Most movements are within five kilometres, but on the east coast they move much greater distances. Locally, we have found that the wider breeding population is reliant upon a few huge winter feeding sites. Some breeding sites are completely deserted in the autumn as birds congregate at the winter sites and then they return in April and May to breed. This means that conservation measures need to be targeted at both winter and summer sites and we inform the landowners that they are not only responsible for the birds on their land but also for those from several kilometres away. Working with farmers we have put up 1,200 nest boxes for Tree Sparrows across north Wiltshire. Farmers have planted hedgerows and conservation crops and created dewponds to provide habitat for sparrows to forage for insects. Together with the farmers we feed over 20 tonnes of grain each year for Tree Sparrows and other farmland birds across 200 square miles.

Across the country, where such conservation measures are implemented and Tree Sparrow populations have not become isolated, their numbers have stabilised and in many cases they are increasing so there is hope yet for this brilliant farmland bird.

CHANGING BOCC STATUS 1–2–3–4

RED-LIST CRITERIA APPLICABLE

- IUCN Globally Threatened
- Historical breeding population decline
- Breeding population decline
- Non-breeding population decline
- Breeding range decline
- Non-breeding range decline

WORDS – MATT PRIOR | **ART –** BETH GARNETT

58

Yellow Wagtail

Motacilla flava

The first Yellow Wagtail of the spring is always a special moment in my birding calendar. My 'safe bet' is a local cereal field, where a late-April visit can reliably produce a male or two – inevitably found perching on the tallest ears of wheat in hopes of attracting a passing female. Watching them, I like to imagine where they've been during our winter – the exotic landscapes they have crossed and the perils they've encountered.

CHANGING BOCC STATUS 1–2–3–4

RED-LIST CRITERIA APPLICABLE
- IUCN Globally Threatened
- Historical breeding population decline
- Breeding population decline
- Non-breeding population decline
- Breeding range decline
- Non-breeding range decline

A few years ago I was lucky enough to get a glimpse into that mysterious window in their lives. It came while I was in a safari bus, within arm's reach of a herd of African Elephants rooting through a steamy swamp. Though I was captivated by the great beasts, the wagtails were the stars of that show – a living carpet of feathered energy that flickered beneath the feet of the herd.

They were a motley bunch – not yet sporting their spring finery – and each had a different shade of grey on the cap, indicating that, like my fellow safari-goers, they were drawn from all corners of Europe. Watching them feast on the insects kicked up by the elephants felt like a glimpse into the distant past. Yellow Wagtails have been seeking out herds of 'megafauna' on the African savannas for countless millennia, taking advantage of the juicy invertebrates they disturb from the torn earth.

Just a few thousand years ago their foraging tactics would have been much the same in Britain, though 'our' Yellow Wagtails would have flocked behind the great beasts of the north – mammoths, Woolly Rhinoceros and Musk Ox, all of which vanished from our shores shortly after the arrival of humans.

To this day, wagtails can still be seen following the biggest beasts in the British landscape – but those beasts are made of metal, and tear the earth in straight lines rather than haphazard lumps. Their wheels still kick up insects from the soil – but every year that bounty is reduced. And these beasts also make their own steam – a greenish, acrid steam that catches in your throat, and leaves the insects dazed and twitching.

The wagtails have been following beasts for millions of years, but I fear they may not be doing it for millions more.

WORDS – JAMES GILROY | **ART –** RUSS HESELDEN

59 Grey Wagtail

Motacilla cinerea

CHANGING BOCC STATUS 1–2–3–4

RED-LIST CRITERIA APPLICABLE

- IUCN Globally Threatened
- Historical breeding population decline
- Breeding population decline
- Non-breeding population decline
- Breeding range decline
- Non-breeding range decline

From a kayak, with something of the human form disguised, it's possible to approach the wild things sharing a river a little more closely, but also much harder to manage binoculars, so the experience cannot be an optically enhanced one. I like it this way, with birds not necessarily the sharp-focussed stars of the show, but accents in the scene as it scrolls by, their calls motifs in the continuous soundscape of rushing water.

This was the way I came to know Dippers, Kingfishers and Grey Herons, often registering them only peripherally as the flow whisked me past: a bobbing white bib, an electric flicker of otherworldly blue, a cold shoulder in shades of grey. Grey Wagtails are different, though. For them, you need to stop. Their small grey backs blend with the rocks. The lemon-meringue undercarriage could be a leaf, prematurely fallen. Even the flicking of a white-edged tail can merge with spits of spume and the semi-rhythmic chop and pulse of the water.

As soon as you pause, they leap into focus and become the centre of everything. This last summer in a deep limestone gorge, close to noon on the hottest day of the year, there was respite in the shade of trees and Ivy clinging to the rocky precipices above; tones of emerald, jade and bronzy blue to soothe the eye. The 'grey wags' were there, perched on mossy rocks, wagging not their tails, but their whole bodies, like pump-handles, and launching intermittent forays to pluck insects from the air. On each spree, they rose almost vertically, as though drawn up on invisible threads by an unseen puppeteer into a brief Tinkerbell bob-hover, white wingbars blurring.

I was only half-watching when one bird flickered upwards to where the gorge walls came closest together. It hung there as a breeze shifted the vegetation above, admitting a steep shaft of sunlight and suddenly I was paying attention with every fibre, because the bird was incandescent – transformed into a creature of air and dancing fire. For an instant a gnat in the same fierce light was golden too: a tiny, floating spark of life. The distance between these two gilded apparitions closed and then the gnat was gone, and the fire went out, and the bird was back in the shade on the rock, wagging, cool as earth and water.

WORDS – AMY-JANE BEER | **ART –** TARA OKON

Tree Pipit

Anthus trivialis

Yarncliffe, in north-east Derbyshire: a rocky margin of moor and scrub that hangs above a gorge thick with old oaks. Its name means 'eagle edge', now only in the imagination, but it's still a place of rare things.

Just below the fringes of the moor, there's an abandoned quarry where birch has swarmed in, laying claim to a couple of the Peak District's best rock climbs. Late in spring, struggling up one of these, I hear birdsong that matches something in my head, the sense of time being stretched: a series of notes, lengthening, winding down, "*whee-wheee-wheeee*", and then ceasing altogether. The small corner of my mind not busy with climbing bursts with joy. It's a Tree Pipit, somewhere over my right shoulder. And then it's off again, fluttering back into the air, a bubbling fanfare bouncing off the surrounding trees as it drifts back to the crowning birches with wings spread, tail flared and legs hanging.

Pipits are often regarded as dreary-looking birds, the avocado bathroom of the avian world. That only makes me love them more, but telling these flecked brown birds apart visually is a task of tooth-grinding attention to detail. The resident Meadow Pipit is a far more common bird with almost two million territories compared to just eighty thousand or so territories for the Tree Pipit, the latter a summer visitor that most commonly breeds in the north and west of Britain. It's a shade bigger, with a thicker bill, and somehow more elegant and more crisply marked than the blurry 'mipit', a bird that seems fretful, fluttering and anxious, as though marked psychologically by the long, dark winter. The Tree Pipit has a touch of swagger, strutting across the ground, tail pumping rhythmically, like a wagtail, as it hunts for insects. It also breeds on the ground, laying half a dozen eggs or so in hidden corners beneath the trees.

Hearing a Tree Pipit is much the easiest way to identify it. The bird's apparent self-confidence is most strongly expressed in song, delivered convincingly in flight or in snatches from the top branches of a tree. Phrases come tumbling out that echo fragments of the Chaffinch song, or the "*jug-jug*" of a Song Thrush. Dialectical variation is strong, partly because of its falling and fragmenting population. The coppiced woodlands of old, perfect habitat for this bird of woodland fringes, are largely gone. It's on the margins, in places like Yarncliffe, where the birds hang on.

CHANGING BOCC STATUS 1–2–3–4

RED-LIST CRITERIA APPLICABLE

- IUCN Globally Threatened
- Historical breeding population decline
- Breeding population decline
- Non-breeding population decline
- Breeding range decline
- Non-breeding range decline

WORDS – ED DOUGLAS | **ART –** STANLEY BIRD

61

Hawfinch

Coccothraustes coccothraustes

It's late November at the walled garden as I turn the key in the heavy paint-flaked door. Damp has settled on the Box hedges, spider webs hang between seedheads of Lovage and Teasel. There's plenty of winter food here for birds to glean amongst the tall herb plants. A scattering of Bramblings and Chaffinches scavenge amongst beechmast and Blackbirds hollow out the apples below the espalier trees.

I follow the gravel path onto dew-wet grass, and there beneath the wall-trained Cherry trees is a bird I've not seen close before. Striking, vivid, exotic looking, it's crushing Cherry stones with its huge triangular beak: a Hawfinch, *Coccothraustes coccothraustes*. The name means 'seed breaker' and it can crack open Plum, Yew and Olive stones or the knuckles of a careless bird ringer.

I've only ever seen Hawfinches high up in the Beech trees, small silhouettes through binoculars. Now on the ground I can study its extraordinary plumage. Head feathers the colour of corten steel. Black bib and black eye surround giving a sharp intent look. A head that looks big for its body, thickset to carry that massive beak. White flashes on wings. Iridescent blue tips to its primaries that, sculpted in the shape of billhooks, overlap like plates of armour. A softly pinkish breast fading to white beneath its tail.

With powerful jaw muscles and that helmet-shaped beak, a Hawfinch can exert a pressure exceeding 50 kilograms. At the back of the jaws is a bony serrated ridge. By wedging a Cherry stone between that and the front of the bill the hard pit can be broken open to eat the nutritious kernel. In summer though, like many other seed-eating birds, Hawfinches turn to insects and soft-bodied caterpillars in the leaf canopy.

There are estimated to be around a thousand breeding pairs of Hawfinch in Britain, these numbers boosted by winter migrants. Though they are twice the size of a Greenfinch their quiet song makes them hard to find in leafy summer. Because they are so difficult to spot, jubilant birdwatchers post sightings on social media.

That moment in the walled garden was 20 years ago. Then, there were known Hawfinch sites in Northumberland, such as Hulne Park at Alnwick. The *Northumberland Bird Atlas* now reports that as breeding birds they are "verging on extinction in the county". That early winter morning in the walled garden has become a poignant memory.

CHANGING BOCC STATUS 1–2–3–4

RED-LIST CRITERIA APPLICABLE

- IUCN Globally Threatened
- Historical breeding population decline
- Breeding population decline
- Non-breeding population decline
- Breeding range decline
- Non-breeding range decline

WORDS – SUSIE WHITE | **ART –** KRYSTEN NEWBY

62

Linnet

Linaria cannabina

CHANGING BOCC STATUS 1–2–3–4

RED-LIST CRITERIA APPLICABLE
- IUCN Globally Threatened
- Historical breeding population decline
- Breeding population decline
- Non-breeding population decline
- Breeding range decline
- Non-breeding range decline

A female Linnet is a typical streaky little brown bird, and I quite like the females, but the gaudy males are, to my mind, one of the least attractive of all UK birds. Now, obviously, opinions will differ on a matter as subjective as physical attractiveness, but the male Linnet is for me the chinless wonder of the bird world – a most inferior finch.

The grey head and rosy breast markings seem to me to resemble a piece of cheap, badly-coloured pottery – the type of thing one might win at a fairground and only keep because it was a prize – an unprized prize. Even the rosy breast markings are a rather tasteless raspberry colour. You may disagree?

But whatever the failings of the male Linnet's plumage, this is a bird which has declined in numbers very dramatically over the last 50 years, as have many other (more attractive) farmland birds and therefore deserves our help because of its plight. Anyone under the age of 30 years won't really have noticed much change in Linnet numbers in their lives but older observers might remember Linnet populations of three times the current numbers. The population decline was steep and sustained during the 1960s, 1970s and 1980s and appears, probably, to have been driven by declines in breeding success throughout that period and beyond, with nest failures at egg and chick stage increasing and clutch size declining.

Linnets are fairly unusual in eating seeds throughout the year (as other finches, buntings and sparrows do mostly in autumn and winter) including in the breeding season; seeds make up by far the largest part of the nestling diet (that's the unusual bit). The seeds come from a wide range of plant species including dandelions, docks, groundsels, chickweeds, Shepherd's Purse and Charlock. Many of these are farmland plants which are either intentionally clobbered by intensive arable farming or end up as collateral damage following herbicide use. It's instructive to spend a few minutes in arable farmland in May pretending to be a Linnet and looking for seeds, or for any chance of there being future seeds, and you'll probably find the pickings are very slight. The solution to the Linnet's population decline is kinder agriculture, and although its ecology is somewhat different from many other declining farmland birds, reform of farming practice is the best chance of seeing more Linnets in the countryside.

WORDS – MARK AVERY | **ART –** NYE HUGHES

63

Twite

Linaria flavirostris

Of all the birds on the British Red List, Twite might well have been one of those you'd not heard of before now. Indeed, they're often given the unenviable title of the 'ultimate birders bird', the ornithological equivalent to 'a face only a mother could love'. Perhaps the only other serious contenders for the title are the Spotted Flycatcher and Garden Warbler. Sadly, the Red-listed former is also featured in this book whilst the latter hardly features in any.

Twite however, are a bird of quiet charm. The scientific name, *Linaria flavirostris* broadly translates to 'resembling linen' or the 'linen-weaver', maybe referring to the yellow ochre wash over the face and neck (a makeup tip, I often think borrowed from another grassland specialist the Grey Partridge), and yellow-billed, obvious only during the winter months. Below an otherwise drab plumage, and after the bill has faded back to pencil-lead grey, some males hide a red wine-stained rump, a badge of status during the breeding season, now increasingly competitive with suitable habitat at a premium.

The bizarre English name is supposedly descriptive of their buzzing "tveeiht" (Twite!) flight call, but perhaps the 'Pennine finch' or the Welsh 'Llinos y Mynydd' ('Linnet of the mountain') are more evocative. As the various names suggest, Twite are associated with in-bye grassland, dry-stone walls and millstone grit, but the species is perhaps better known to most as a winter visitor to coastal mudflats and salt marshes. Once numbering several thousand, these winter flocks rarely reach double figures and often, now, only single birds return to once well-known sites.

I've been lucky enough to work on Twite, following them individually to learn about their ecology, demography and survival. For me, they represent the last of England's wilderness accessible by bus from Manchester, Sheffield and Leeds – a distant call, half-heard in windswept hill country is enough.

Across Europe, their decline is probably tied to changes in upland farming practices and intensive moorland management, but the warming climate and the changing coastal landscape are also likely to be contributing factors. Restoration of upland meadows, supplementary feeding and ongoing colour-ringing of what small and fragmented populations remain have helped Twite in the UK and Ireland, but sadly, have so far failed to stabilise their decline. Perhaps most worrying however is our own current lack of knowledge, and that a species once so familiar could disappear without anybody really noticing at all.

CHANGING BOCC STATUS 1–2–3–4

RED-LIST CRITERIA APPLICABLE

- IUCN Globally Threatened
- Historical breeding population decline
- Breeding population decline
- Non-breeding population decline
- Breeding range decline
- Non-breeding range decline

WORDS – JAMIE DUNNING | **ART –** WILLIAM NEILL

WNeill

Lesser Redpoll

Acanthis cabaret

CHANGING BOCC STATUS 1–2–3–4

RED-LIST CRITERIA APPLICABLE
- IUCN Globally Threatened
- Historical breeding population decline
- Breeding population decline
- Non-breeding population decline
- Breeding range decline
- Non-breeding range decline

Some birds slip under the radar. The Lesser Redpoll is one. Seen well, the male's breast and forehead glow like blusher. Usually though, this is a bird that hides its charms. Not dull, exactly – no living thing deserves to be called that – and 'LBJ' ('little brown job') is a bit of birdish that always makes me shudder. But discreet, sure. The Redpoll is one of those species that, unless we focus, make an effort, tends to pass us by.

This small and streaky bird also has the misfortune of being a finch. The finch family is full of extroverts, with their fancy bills, mellifluous songs and 'look-at-me' display flights. Most of them pout on calendars, greetings-cards, magazine covers; the Redpoll, not so much.

As if that were not enough, ornithologists have spent the past few decades debating what a Redpoll actually is. Various European and North American forms of Redpoll have been lumped together as the same species, split into subspecies, then lumped and split again so many times, by so many people, that it's easy to obsess over labels and names on a list, losing sight of them as creatures with an existence independent of ours. Once, the form that breeds in Britain was known as the 'Red-headed Linnet'. Today, it's the 'Lesser Redpoll' (or 'Common Redpoll' in Ireland), which rather rubs the poor bird's face in it. For all the taxonomic confusion, it is no less a redpoll.

My own listing days are long behind me – often I don't even pick up binoculars when heading out for a stroll. Plenty has been written about this more mindful approach to enjoying nature but, suffice to say, I now notice more. I certainly notice more Redpolls. It helps that, since we swapped Hackney for Somerset's Quantock Hills, my study has looked onto a pair of handsome Silver Birches as tall as our house. Birches lure Redpolls like moths to flame, and so every winter our rural garden is graced by these gregarious little birds.

Clinging to the flimsiest twigs, frequently upside-down, these industrious finches extract tiny seeds from the catkins with barely-there bills. They have a habit of holding down a catkin with one leg, parrot-style, while working away. Meantime, their wheezy chattering – such a cheery sound – comes from all around the trees. Sometimes they are joined by Siskins and the odd Bullfinch, and their calls mingle, joyously. I feel blessed.

WORDS – BEN HOARE | **ART –** JOHN THRELFALL

John Threlfall

Yellowhammer

Emberiza citrinella

CHANGING BOCC STATUS 1–2–3–4

RED-LIST CRITERIA APPLICABLE

- IUCN Globally Threatened
- Non-breeding population decline
- Historical breeding population decline
- Breeding range decline
- Breeding population decline
- Non-breeding range decline

One of my earliest memories from when I was a child is going to a place called Marshfield, an area of farmland filled with crops just into Gloucestershire, with my parents and sister. It was a nice day trip and a simple adventure; we used to frequent it quite often, on the search for Quail on summer evenings but never getting more than a few seconds of its enigmatic call.

But this day we weren't looking for Quail, but for a flock of Yellowhammers. They had become very scarce where I lived in the Chew Valley, less than an hour away. They were more common in Marshfield, often singing their characteristic song, "*a little bit of bread and no cheese*".

Yellowhammers are medium-sized buntings, the male is mainly yellow, at least on the head and underside, as the name suggests. They can congregate in large flocks, even by the roadside, and used to be common countryside birds but have been badly affected by habitat loss due to modern farming practices.

One of the things I love to do is ringing birds, which is one of the ways scientific data are collected by the British Trust for Ornithology. I received my ringing licence at Chew Valley Ringing Station when I reached 16 and love to ring in my garden, but have never ringed a Yellowhammer at home. Each winter we visit a farm near Bath, to ring Yellowhammers. They are absolutely beautiful birds and in the hand they are one of my favourites.

Yellowhammer numbers have gone into free fall since the war and the species is now a Red-listed Bird of Conservation Concern.

Last autumn I was making a TV documentary about the decline of grassland and farmland bird species and interviewed Professor Kevin Gaston from Exeter University, who told me that there were 400 million fewer birds in Europe compared to just 30 years ago. As part of that filming I also visited RSPB's Hope Farm, where they have been making simple changes to their farming practices and monitoring the impact. Here Yellowhammer numbers have increased by 80%. I also interviewed Martin Lines from Nature Friendly Farming Network who told me a similar story. These interviews have given me hope for the future of Yellowhammers.

I hope that by the time I am birding with my children the Yellowhammer will be out of danger and a common sight in our countryside once again.

WORDS – MYA-ROSE CRAIG | **ART –** BEN WOODHAMS

Cirl Bunting

Emberiza cirlus

CHANGING BoCC STATUS 1–2–3–4

RED-LIST CRITERIA APPLICABLE

- IUCN Globally Threatened
- Historical breeding population decline
- Breeding population decline
- Non-breeding population decline
- Breeding range decline
- Non-breeding range decline

Cirl Bunting (pronounced "sirl") are modest, sedentary birds. They nest close to the ground, well hidden in prickly scrub, favouring thorn and gorse. Males emit a monotonous trill, the sound of a sewing machine rattling down a hem. There's an abrupt pause as if the cloth is being adjusted, and then it's off again, "*zrrrrr*". The call note is a sharp "*zit*".

While the females look like smudged Yellowhammers, males sport handsome yellow collars, which stand out against olive feathering on the breast like the neck ring on a Grass Snake, another creature of untidy meadowland.

Cirl Buntings are regarded as a conservation success story: back from the brink of extinction in Britain, numbers up by a massive 800% in 10 years, reintroduced populations breeding in new territories. Efforts by the RSPB and individual farmers have been fantastic. But the Cirl Bunting's tale is not really a success story – it's a lesson in the consequences of habitat destruction.

In the 1980s, this common farmland bird, once widespread across the south, was reduced to 118 pairs. Most of these were in a narrow coastal strip of southern Devon. Today there are about 1,000 breeding pairs – mostly still living in that same narrow coastal strip, plus some small pockets of Cornwall. These are the remnants of a range that once stretched to North Wales, with outliers in Cumbria.

Numbers started declining from the 1930s, plunging in the 1970s. Modern farming methods caused this devastation by eradicating weedy winter stubbles and grasshopper-rich summer meadows. Cirls were especially vulnerable to the changes because they weren't able to expand their foraging range. Pairs spend their lives in one small zone, moving no more than a mile between breeding and wintering areas. They are each dependent on the features of a specific place: *this* hedge, *that* meadow.

Reduce the land's diversity and you lose not only Cirl Buntings but also other birds, mammals, reptiles, amphibians, plants and insects, all connected in a web of belonging. Some of these creatures may be able to adapt, or go elsewhere. Many cannot. Seen this way, the Cirl Bunting is more than an avian species. It is a fugitive spirit of place, an emblem of a lost *genius loci* that we have un-homed from its haunts. Its ghost is fading as we gradually forget how rich and abundant our common countryside used to be.

WORDS – SARA HUDSTON | **ART –** ROBERT GREENHALF

Robert Greenhalf

Corn Bunting

Emberiza calandra

The arresting snatches of song that drew us across a farm field reminded me of an old fruit seller on the town's long defunct market. Not for him the relentless patter of persuasion. He was a one-liner man, his shout-outs timed with measured deliberation: "Straw-breez! Straw-breez!"

So it was with the Corn Bunting. Three or four Skylarks down among the barley and up there in heaven sang high in ceaseless trills, but the bunting's voice rose clear and higher still. Sitting out on the wires over the field, he threw out his catchphrase – a jingling jingle, a shuffle of notes that stuttered into life, reached a fevered climax, then subsided into a silence of expectation. The expectation that he would sing it again. And again.

Some say this three-second burst sounds like breaking glass. Others insist on the jangling of keys. A close handful of small brass keys, shaken loose. The song's compressed effervescence is addictive, so addictive.

I got my first fix this spring through the car window. That song was sharp enough to pierce the glass. Every week, on the same route, at the exact same spot, the window wound down for maximum effect. Once I walked out to seek its song post. It wasn't hard to find; it never is. This bird on a stick, the leafless, bark-stripped topmost twig of a lone elm bush, where it wanted to be seen. Rotund body fixed bolt upright, head tipped back, lower mandible open so far it appeared half-dislocated, it poured out its scratchy heart. And in the closed beak moments between, its watchful head ratcheted left, left, left, in 40-degree clicks, then back again to the right; click, click, click.

The Corn Bunting is a found and lost kind of bird. Against a national trend of decline, I found buntings singing on five of my local patches a few summers ago. I got to know their favoured perches, the show-and-hear spots where I could entertain delighted visitors. But this year they were lost altogether from all but one of those places. Nobody yet can explain why Corn Buntings come and go from farm fields when there are no discernible changes in habitat. One thing is certain however: in our lifetimes there have been more lost than found. Bye baby bunting? Surely not.

CHANGING BOCC STATUS 1–2–3–4

RED-LIST CRITERIA APPLICABLE

- IUCN Globally Threatened
- Historical breeding population decline
- Breeding population decline
- Non-breeding population decline
- Breeding range decline
- Non-breeding range decline

WORDS – DEREK NIEMANN | **ART –** NICK DERRY

DERRY!

In memoriam

Since the last review of the Red List of Birds of Conservation Concern in 2009, the following three species are now designated as being extinct as breeding species in the UK: Temminck's Stint, Wryneck and Serin.

The last successful breeding attempt by Temminck's Stint was in 1993, but birds have been seen singing and displaying in suitable habitat on a number of occasions since then. This was always a very rare breeding bird here, its tiny Scottish population set somewhat apart from the Arctic breeding grounds used by the species across Scandinavia and Russia.

The Wryneck was once a common bird across England and Wales, its breeding range extending north to the Lake District. Numbers appear to have been in decline since the early 1800s, the breeding range contracting southwards, and by the 1980s only a handful of pairs was reported annually. For a short while it looked as if a small breeding population might become established in Scotland, where the first breeding record was documented in 1969. However, despite the presence of occasional singing males in the north of Scotland, the last confirmed breeding attempt was made in Ross-shire in 2002; the last confirmed breeding in England was in Buckinghamshire in 1985.

Although the Serin is a common breeding bird in continental Europe, with a breeding range that has been expanding northwards, the last confirmed UK breeding was in 2003, when a pair bred in Norfolk. Jersey was host to regular nesting attempts from the 1970s to the 1990s, but the last breeding attempt in the Channel Isles was in 2001. The prospect of future breeding attempts may be wishful thinking perhaps, but the occurrence of birds at suitable sites leaves the door open somewhat.

WORDS – MIKE TOMS | **ART –** STEW GRAHAM

Temminck's Stint

Calidris temminckii

Wryneck

Jynx torquilla

Serin

Serinus serinus

The contributors

NICK ACHESON lives where he grew up, in North Norfolk. Here, from a flint cottage by a duckpond, he walks far and wide, and he thinks and writes on nature.

LIZA ADAMCZEWSKI is an artist and illustrator who studied at Camberwell and The Royal College of Art. Living and working in Pembrokeshire, her work is inspired by the environment. www.lizaadamczewski.com

CARRY AKROYD is a painter-printmaker living between the Nene Valley and the Fens, both of which provide much of her subject matter. www.carryakroyd.co.uk

RICHARD ALLEN is based amid the Essex creeks and marshes, sketching birds in the field, producing linocut collections, together with oils/watercolours of birds and habitats. www.richardallenillustrator.com

MAX ANGUS's linocuts have been exhibited at the SWLA annual exhibition and also as part of 'The Discerning Eye Exhibition' in London. Her artwork also features in a wide range of magazines.

ATM paints huge images of endangered species on urban walls, to bring awareness of their disappearance into the public domain and inspire a desire to protect them. www.atmstreetart.com

MARK AVERY thinks, writes and campaigns about environmental issues. Twitter: @markavery Blog: www.markavery.info/blog

NICK BAKER is a naturalist, broadcaster and writer with a lifelong passion for wildlife of all kinds, especially insects. When he's not bugging he's birding on Dartmoor. www.nick@nickbaker.tv

PATRICK BARKHAM is an award-winning author and the *Guardian's* Natural History Writer. His latest book, *Wild Child*, is about children and nature. patrick.barkham@theguardian.com

SIMON BARNES, author of the *Bad Birdwatcher* trilogy, has just completed *The History of the World in 100 Animals*. Four Cranes once flew over his garden.

AMY-JANE BEER is a biologist, naturalist, author, columnist, and *Guardian* Country Diarist, thankful not to have to choose between her love of words and her passion for the natural world. @AmyJaneBeer

NATALIE BENNETT is a British politician and journalist, who was born and raised in Australia. She is a former leader of the Green Party of England and Wales and is a graduate of agricultural science..

STANLEY BIRD is a Scottish artist based in Edinburgh painting funky animals and birds with a bold palette in acrylics and mixed media. www.stanleybird.co.uk

COLIN BLANCHARD is a printmaker, making original editions in linocut and screenprint. Now living in south-west Scotland, he has a previous career in countryside education.

ALEX BOND is the Senior Curator in charge of birds at the Natural History Museum in Tring where he studies the conservation of island and marine birds.

APITHANNY BOURNE is a Scottish entomologist and artist. In her free time, she likes to paint threatened species to raise money and awareness for conservation charities. www.heliconius.earth

DAN BRADBURY studied technical illustration and now works as Director of Communications and Development at the World Land Trust. www.danbradburyart.co.uk

KEITH BROCKIE is a wildlife artist whose work has been widely published. He lives with his wife Hazel on the shores of Loch Tay, Perthshire, where he has a studio and gallery. www.keithbrockie.co.uk

MARCO BRODDE lives on an island in the middle of the Wadden Sea. The spectacular landscapes, formed by water, wind and sand, together with the island's wildlife, provide the motivation for his art.

JO BROWN is a professional illustrator from South Devon. Working from her home studio in Teignmouth she illustrates the natural world, working mainly with pen and ink, Karismas, and Copic markers.

MALCOLM BURGESS is a Principal Conservation Scientist at the RSPB Centre for Conservation Science and runs PiedFly.Net, a citizen science network coordinating hole-nesting bird monitoring and research.

TOM CADWALLENDER is an enthusiastic Northumbrian birdwatcher, ringer and BTO Regional Rep. who enjoys the coast, taking photographs and communicating about birds. @tomcadwallender

NICOLA CHESTER is a nature writer, long-standing columnist for RSPB and a school librarian, who seeks to engage people with wildlife whatever she's doing. www.nicolachester.wordpress.com

IAN MICHAEL CLAXTON lives in East Anglia and is a designer and artist, who creates paintings and drawings of wildlife, landscape and nature.

ANN CLEEVES is an English crime-writer, best known for her novels set in Shetland and Northumberland. In 2016, Ann celebrated the publication of 30 books in 30 years. www.anncleeves.com

ANDY CLEMENTS is a nature conservationist and CEO of the British Trust for Ornithology (BTO), dividing time his between Cambridge and Norfolk, work and birding. @_AndyClements

MARK COCKER is an author of creative non-fiction and *Guardian* columnist. His last four works have been shortlisted for nine awards, winning two and, most recently, the East Anglian Book Award (2019).

MARY COLWELL is a producer and writer specialising in natural history. She worked at the BBC Natural History Unit making documentaries for TV and Radio and has written two books. Her third is due in 2020.

DOMINIC COUZENS is one of Britain's best known writers on birds and nature. He has written several best-selling books and is a columnist in various magazines. He also travels widely as a writer and tour leader.

ROB COWEN is an award-winning writer and author of *Common Ground*, hailed as redefining writing on people and place and voted third in a poll to find Britain's favourite nature book of all time. www.robcowen.net

MYA-ROSE CRAIG is a prominent young conservationist passionate about birds, who campaigns for ethnic diversity in conservation, and organises nature camps for inner-city teenagers.

CROW ARTIST (KIRSTY YEOMANS) believes that illustration is still a strong contender for storytelling, sharing our thoughts and ideas in a world of mass information. www.crowartist.co.uk

CAROLINE DALY is inspired by natural history illustrations and Art Deco artists, all mixed up with a love for geometry and all things symmetrical. She especially likes drawing things with wings. www.carolinedaly.co.uk

LIZZIE DALY is a welsh wildlife biologist, broadcaster, film-maker and conservationist, with a healthy curiosity for the natural world that has led her to conduct research and make films all over the world.

FYFE DANGERFIELD – founding member of kaleido-pop band Guillemots – is a British musician and songwriter. He recently launched the "everything & anything" station www.channelsmaychange.com

MIRIAM DARLINGTON is a prize-winning poet and writer, author of *Otter Country* and *Owl Sense*. She lectures in creative writing at Plymouth University and writes for *The Countryman* and *Resurgence-Ecologist*.

DAVID DARRELL-LAMBERT is Director of Bird Brain UK and has been addicted to birds since he was nine. Four decades later, he is still mad about them and addicted to nocturnal bird migration across the capital

NICK DERRY lives in Besançon, France, and divides his time between sketching wildlife in the field and playing with those memories and images in the studio. www.nickderry.webs.com

MIKE DILGER has been an obsessive naturalist since childhood; he is now best known for his regular appearances as the 'wild man' on BBC1's *The One Show*. www.mikedilger.co.uk @dilgertv

ED DOUGLAS is a climber and nature writer living in Sheffield. His latest book is *Kinder Scout: The People's Mountain*, which includes photographs by John Beatty. @calmandfearless

JAMIE DUNNING is an easily-distracted ornithologist, interested in Twite. His PhD, on avian sociality, focusses on another small brown bird, the House Sparrow.

MARK EATON is a Principal Conservation Scientist in the RSPB Centre for Conservation Science, working on surveys, red-lists, indicators and 'state of' reporting.

LEO DU FEU is a Scottish artist of landscape and nature, trained at Edinburgh College of Art. He volunteers for BTO surveys and has had two books published. www.leodufeu.co.uk.

TOM FINCH is a Conservation Scientist at the RSPB, interested in agriculture, climate change and bird migration.

JOHN FOKER lives in a former mining village in County Durham. He seeks to encapsulate the whole experience of a wildlife encounter rather than a single moment. www.bearparkartists.co.uk

TIFFANY FRANCIS-BAKER is a writer and illustrator from the South Downs. Her third book *Dark Skies* was published with Bloomsbury in 2019. www.tiffanyfrancisbaker.com

KATIE FULLER has been fascinated by wildlife, especially birds, for as long as she can remember. She also developed a love of drawing and making things. www.katiefuller.co.uk

KERRIE ANN GARDNER is a photographer and illustrator who lives nestled within the beautiful borderlands of Dorset, Devon and Somerset. www.kerrieanngardner.co.uk

JACKIE GARNER uses acrylics and watercolours to depict wildlife. She is a teacher, tour leader and author of *The Wildlife Artist's Handbook*. www.jackiegarner.co.uk

BETH GARNETT is an artist and maker living in Cornwall. Her colourful, playful work often features animal characters and a touch of humour. www.bethgarnett.com

BEN GARROD is Professor of Evolutionary Biology and Science Engagement at the University of East Anglia. He is also an award-wining BBC natural history presenter and author. www.bengarrod.co.uk

DICK GILHESPY's interest in wildlife began with primary school wildlife walks; it has never left him. Watching and sketching birds is important to Dick. @citybirding1

SIMON GILLINGS is a keen birder, artist, photographer and sound recordist. He works at BTO, lives in Cambridge, but escapes to the coast to watch waders, seabirds and migrants at every opportunity.

JAMES GILROY is a Lecturer in Ecology at University of East Anglia. Having studied Yellow Wagtails for his PhD, his research now explores human impacts on bird species worldwide.

FIONA GOMEZ is an ex-Warner Bros Animation artist who became a carer, got lost, then found sketching birds in Northumberland. Art Outdoors Therapy 07743 595567 flickr.com/photos/figomez

STEW GRAHAM is a graphic designer, birder and co-founder of the Probable Bird Society. If you need him he'll be at Whittle Dene yelling at dog walkers. @stewpottery www.graphic-stew.co.uk

HOWARD GRAY is a children's illustrator. He works digitally, but loves to incorporate watercolour washes and textures wherever he can to give his illustrations a painterly quality. www.howardgrayillustrations.com

ROBERT GREENHALF lives in East Sussex, working mainly in oils and woodcut. His inspiration comes from the nearby Romney Marsh, but he also travels widely. www.robertgreenhalf.co.uk

SARAH HARRIS is a fanatical birder, rapt by migration and rarer bird ID. She started ringing as a kid and today juggles the BTO/JNCC/RSPB Breeding Bird Survey and fieldwork at BTO.

MELISSA HARRISON is a novelist and nature writer, whose novel *All Among the Barley* was named as the UK winner of the European Union Prize for Literature. www.melissaharrison.co.uk

RUSS HESELDEN paints the everyday wildlife of Norfolk. He sketches outdoors as much as possible and works in ink, watercolour and oil. www.russheselden.co.uk

BEN HOARE was Features Editor for *BBC Wildlife* for 10 years, winning the BTO's Dilys Breese Medal. He is now a freelance magazine journalist and bestselling children's author. www.benhoare.com

SARA HUDSTON is a writer living in the rural west of Dorset. www.sarahudston.co.uk

NYE HUGHES is an artist and designer based in Edinburgh. He draws inspiration from the landscape, plants and seabird cliffs of coastal Scotland. www.nyehughes.co.uk.

KIT JEWITT is a birder and part-time conservationist from Northumberland. He co-founded 'Probable Bird Society', is a *Springwatch* 'Unsprung Hero' and has appeared on *Tweet of the Day* on Radio 4.

RICHARD JOHNSON is based in Cambridge, getting out into the countryside as much as he can to paint and sketch wildlife. Search for 'Richard Johnson – Wildlife Artist' on Facebook for news of his work.

KITTIE JONES is drawn to the diverse Scottish landscape. She makes mixed-media drawings and prints documenting her experience of nature. www.kittiejones.com

ED KEEBLE is a birder and bird artist based in Suffolk. He seeks to capture birds 'in the moment' and uses a wide range of media, including digital painting.

MARTIN KETCHER is a birder and conservation volunteer; since 2011 he has spent each summer at RSPB Geltsdale monitoring Whinchats. He works as the Water Vole Conservation Officer for HMWT.

SZABOLCS KÓKAY is an illustrator, wildlife artist and nature painter, based in Hungary. He regularly takes part in international exhibitions and competitions, including the SWLA's 'Natural Eye' show in London.

MIRANDA KRESTOVNIKOFF is a radio and television presenter specialising in natural history and archaeological programmes. www.mirandak.co.uk

BELLA LACK is a 17-year old environmental activist, writer and (soon to be) presenter.

ROB LAMBERT is an environment academic, birder, broadcaster and expedition ship lecturer, based at the University of Nottingham.

ALEXANDER LEES is a Senior Lecturer in biodiversity at Manchester Metropolitan University, UK and a research associate of the Cornell Lab of Ornithology, Cornell University, USA.

WYNONA LEGG is based in Devon. She was elected an Associate member of the SWLA in 2019 and won the Larson Juhl award in the same year. www.wynonalegg.com

GILL LEWIS is a children's author, vet and treehouse dweller, writing about the wild world and our human relationship with it. www.gilllewis.com

DAVID LINDO (The Urban Birder) is a broadcaster, writer, speaker and tour leader, who seeks to engage people with the natural environment through the medium of birds. www.theurbanbirderworld.com

JOHN LLOYD is predominantly a wildlife artist with birds his favourite subject. He is a keen birder who enjoys frequenting his local reserves at Hengistbury Head and Stanpit Marsh, near Christchurch in Dorset.

KAREN LLOYD is a writer and activist. Her two books, *The Gathering Tide; a Journey Around the Edgelands of Morecambe Bay* and *The Blackbird Diaries*, both award winners, are published by Saraband.

TIM MACKRILL is a conservationist and writer, working on Osprey and White-tailed Eagle reintroductions and other species recovery projects.

LUKE MASSEY is an award winning wildlife photographer and cameraman with a passion for birds. He spent much of 2019 working on his upcoming documentary, '*The Last Song of the Nightingale*'.

RORY McCANN studied zoology and conservation in his younger years., which fuelled his passion for painting wildlife. He has been working as a mural artist for the last seven years.

DARA McANULTY is a naturalist, conservationist and passionate advocate for wildlife, the youngest ever recipient of the RSPB Medal for services to nature conservation. @NaturalistDara

LUCY McROBERT is wildlife storyteller, nature writer, communicator and author of *365 Days Wild* (2019). She freelances in marketing for nature charities. www.365dayswild.com

EMMA MITCHELL is a naturalist and author, writing about the ways in which contact with nature can improve mental health and well-being.

STEPHEN MOSS is a naturalist, author and broadcaster. He is President of the Somerset Wildlife Trust, and teaches travel and nature writing at Bath Spa University.

EMMA MURRAY is an artist from Lancashire, UK and currently lives and teaches biology in Colorado, USA. Her Ph.D. explored the wintering and migratory ecology of Whinchats in Nigeria.

WILLIAM NEILL is a resident of South Uist, who chose Twite to illustrate because they are one of the few small birds to stay and are always a joy to see on a cold winter's day. www.william-neill.co.uk

KRYSTEN NEWBY works and lives in rural Bury St Edmunds, Suffolk, surrounded by her beloved wildlife. She is a wildlife artist, graphic designer and ethical taxidermist. www.krysthecreator.com

ADAM NICOLSON is the author of *Sea Room* and *The Seabird's Cry*, two books which draw their life from the Shiant Isles in the Outer Hebrides.

DEREK NIEMANN is an author, feature writer, editor, *Guardian* Country Diarist and creative writing tutor at Cambridge University. www.whispersfromthewild.co.uk

TARA OKON lives in Pontypridd and works as an environmental educator. She studied graphic design in the early 1990's but has only relatively recently returned to her love of drawing.

JAMES O'NEILL is a lover of all wildlife, but especially birds and insects. Although based in Cork, his home is Co. Armagh. James runs @Irishwoodcock and is an artist and photographer. @Jamesoneillii

CHRIS ORGILL is a painter & illustrator based in North Norfolk. Inspired by wildlife and landscape, his work is the result of sketches and paintings made from observations and encounters in the field. @chris_orgill

CHRIS PACKHAM talks and writes about wildlife, photographs it and spends a lot of time trying to help look after it, something which seems to get him into trouble. But he doesn't care about that.

LISA PANNEK is a freelance illustrator and artist based in Kiel, Germany. Since her early childhood she has been in love with birds, especially raptors. www.lisapannek.com

LEV PARIKIAN loved birds when he was a child, then ignored them for a shamefully long time, then loved them again. When he was 50, he wrote a book telling that exact story, but with more words.

JIM PERRIN is a nature writer and the *Guardian's* Country Diarist for Wales. In earlier years he was a leading British rock-climber.

JONATHAN POMROY is a North Yorkshire wildlife and landscape artist painting in watercolour and oils. He is also the author of *On Crescent Wings – a Portrait of the Swift*. www.jonathanpomroy.co.uk

ADELE POUND is a wildlife artist and keen birdwatcher based in Northern Ireland. The recipient of several awards and bursaries, her work is part of many private collections. www.adelepound.co.uk

MATT PRIOR is passionate about birds and conservation, using bird ringing to learn more. He specialises in farmland birds and in improving habitats for birds in Wiltshire. @mattthesparrow

JONNY RANKIN lives for nature and thrives in the great outdoors. Through his love of nature he volunteers, fundraises, writes, and – on occasion – give talks. www.jonnyrankin.co.uk

DARREN REES was born in Hampshire in 1961 and his work has attracted many awards, most recently the Artist in Residency honour from the Friends of the Scott Polar Research Institute.

TRISTAN REID is a lifelong conservationist, naturalist and passionate birder, also known as 'The Inked Naturalist' because of his many bird tattoos. These were part of his project to raise funds for conservation.

IAN RENDALL lives in Aberdeenshire and is a watercolour wildlife artist with a passion for birds. He is an ornithologist and bird ringer, continually inspired by the natural world. @IRendall

ALICE RISELY is an academic researcher at the University of Ulm, Germany, studying wildlife microbiology. She spent two months monitoring Aquatic Warbler nests in Poland in 2011.

DEREK ROBERTSON exhibits around the world and his paintings are held in collections in more than 50 countries, including those of HRH the Duke of Edinburgh and The Tate Gallery. www.derekrobertson.com

WILL ROSE is a British animator, illustrator and wildlife fan. He currently works as a designer on the BAFTA Award winning children's series '*Hey Duggee*' and directs his own short films. www.willswork.co.uk

RAY SCALLY is widely published in many books and journals in the UK and internationally and is widely known as the illustrator for the *Birding Frontiers* Challenge Series of seasonal bird identification guides.

DAFILA SCOTT After working as a zoologist, Dafila Scott turned to drawing and painting. Her current work includes figurative and abstract paintings inspired by the natural world. www.dafilascott.co.uk

CAIN SCRIMGEOUR is a naturalist, film-maker, photographer, lecturer at the University of Cumbria and Media Director and Expedition Leader at Wild Intrigue. www.wildintrigue.co.uk

CARL SEEBODE has lived throughout Europe and Asia, but currently lives and works in Birmingham. He studied Fine Art at BIAD and has since been working full-time as an art teacher. @sec_462

MATT SEWELL, artist, illustrator and avid ornithologist, is a regular contributor to the *Caught By The River* website and author of bestselling books. He has illustrated for the *Guardian*, Barbour and others.

MATT SHARDLOW is Chief Executive of Buglife – the Invertebrate Conservation Group – and Country Diary columnist in the *Guardian*; he is also a member of the BBC Rural Affairs Committee

SUZY SHARPE is a Cornwall-based painter of birds with a fresh contemporary twist inspired by poetry, narrative and the experience of wildlife in a busy world.

JANE SMITH is a printmaker from the west coast of Scotland. She won the Birdwatch/Swarovski Artist of the Year 2015, and is author of *Wild Island*. www.janesmithwildlifeart.blogspot.com

CLAIRE STARES is a writer, conservationist and *Guardian* country diarist. Passionate about wildlife and wild places, she divides her time between Hampshire and the Scottish Highlands.

RACHEL C. TAYLOR is an ornithologist and bird ringer based in Snowdonia. Rachel's bird sculptures take a non-traditional approach to copper-foiled stained glass. www.delweddyfran.com

PAUL THOMAS is now the political cartoonist of the *Daily Mail*, having previously held the post at the Daily Express. His book *A Tabloid History of Birdwatching* was published in 2018. www.paulthomascartoons.co.uk

STEPH' THORPE has been a birder and artist for over 35 years, and has a special interest in painting the avian waifs and strays that visit the UK from afar.

JOHN THRELFALL is based in Scotland. Field drawings in watercolour or pastel pencil are the basis for all his work, though preferring pastel, acrylic or oils in the studio. www.johnthrelfall.co.uk

RUTH TINGAY is an award-winning conservationist, who has studied birds of prey on five continents. Since 2010 she has been campaigning against the illegal persecution of birds of prey in the UK.

RACHEL TOLL is one of the West Country's leading wildlife water colourists, with a highly individual style developed without formal training. If people like what she has painted, then that makes her very happy.

MIKE TOMS is a science communicator and ornithologist working at BTO. He has authored a number of books, including two in the Collins *New Naturalist* series, and volunteers as a nest recorder and ringer.

NATALIE TOMS is a self-taught wildlife artist from Lanlivery in Cornwall. She creates from her artist studio at the bottom of the garden. www.natalietoms.com

LIZ TOOLE is a painter and printmaker, showing her work in galleries all over the UK. In the future Liz would love to work alongside The RSPB and or BTO on an Artists Residency. www.liztoole.co.uk

EMILY TULL's artwork is inspired by everyday life and literature, her wildlife work particularly focusses on species that are dwindling in numbers. www.emilytull.co.uk

ROBERT VAUGHAN is an Irish freelance wildlife artist and illustrator, combining his love of art and passion for birds and nature. www.robertvaughanillustrations.com

HANNAH WARD is the RSPB's Area Manager in Beds, Cambs and Herts. Hannah has a background in species recovery and reintroductions.

SAMUEL WEST is an actor and theatre director, who has worked across theatre, television, film and radio, and as reciter with orchestras – performing at the Last Night of the Proms in 2002. @exitthelemming

SUSIE WHITE is a gardener, nature writer and *Guardian* Country Diarist, living in a North Pennine valley where she has created a garden rich in wildlife. www.susie-white.co.uk

IOLO WILLIAMS is one of the UK's best known nature and wildlife presenters. With a degree in ecology, and a career that began working for the RSPB, he currently presents on *Springwatch* and *Autumnwatch*.

SASKIA WISCHNEWSKI is a conservation scientist working for RSPB, who specialises in the ecology of seabirds, including shearwaters. @saswisch

BEN WOODHAMS is an English artist and illustrator living and working on the Danish island of Bornholm in the Baltic Sea. His practice is founded in direct observation. www.benwoodhams.com

DARREN WOODHEAD is a pure field painter based in East Lothian. A graduate of the Royal College of Art, he works direct in brush and watercolour outside: there is no studio. www.darrenwoodhead.com

ROB YARHAM is an author, editor and photographer who has loved birds all his life, and has watched, studied and written about them for many years. www.robyarham.com

Acknowledgements

This book would not have been possible without the generous contributions of the amazing writers and artists who have given their time, enthusiasm and creative skills for free. We are extremely grateful for their support and kindness.

Kit would particularly like to thank Mike Toms at BTO for his guidance, patience and hard work in ensuring that idea became reality. Thank you to Mark Eaton at the RSPB for the initial inspiration. Special thanks too to the early adopters of the project, and those whose passionate support helped to get it off the ground; Chris Packham, Jamie Dunning, Ben Garrod and Jo Sarsby Management, Derek Niemann, Amy-Jane Beer, Nicola Chester, Lev Parikian and Robert Macfarlane.

On behalf of the contributors we would also like to thank Simon Pawsey of Cairngorms Birding, Carolyn Robertson of Cairngorms National Park, Kevin Rylands, the RSPB Geltsdale site manager Stephen Westerberg and Amanda Proud.

Index

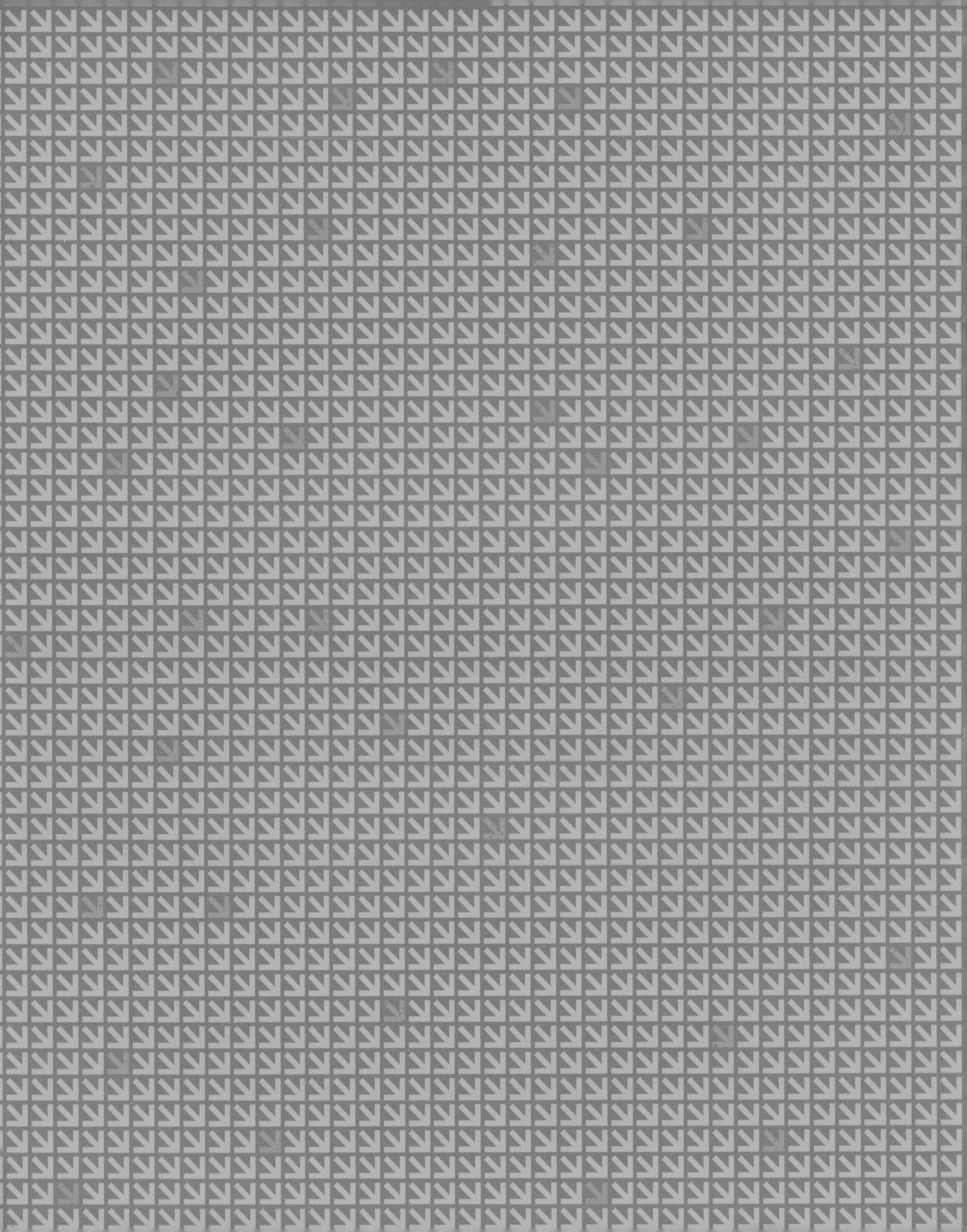